A CANDLE FOR THE DARK

To my father

ANDREW JACKSON ICE
who has been both parents
to me since I was nine

A CANDLE FOR THE DARK

ORVA LEE ICE

ABINGDON PRESS

NEW YORK   NASHVILLE

A CANDLE FOR THE DARK

Copyright MCMLV by Pierce & Washabaugh

Library of Congress Catalog Card Number: 55-8610

SET UP, PRINTED, AND BOUND BY THE
PARTHENON PRESS, AT NASHVILLE,
TENNESSEE, UNITED STATES OF AMERICA

CONTENTS

5

1

THE CALL OF THE BELL

BRUCE MET ME AT THE STATION AND TOOK MY BAG. "Here is Old Betsy," he said, and tugged at the car door, which complainingly squeaked on its unwilling hinges. We rode through the afternoon haze of the countryside. He drove by his church, and we stopped a moment. It was a white frame building fashioned after the colonial pattern. He told me it was more than a hundred years old.

Beth had supper ready when we came in; it was made even more appetizing by her radiant personality. I had had a long journey and was somewhat travel weary, so we all went to bed early. Next day was Sunday, and I was to take Bruce's pulpit.

As is my habit, I awoke early, arose, and prepared myself and dressed. I sat familiarizing myself with my sermon notes on "The Ethical Implications of Worship," when upon my ear fell "the voice of the church." It had been a long time since I had heard it, and the euphony brought a soul-lifting reverence upon me. I opened my door so that the sound might fill my room. I stepped out upon the porch, and as one hungry to hear more, I found myself drawn to the church. I felt like singing for joy and weeping in appreciation at the same time. I walked toward the church and stood

7

in the vestry watching the sexton as he rhythmically pulled upon the rope. He stopped too soon.

"Nothing sounds out the dignity of God," I murmured, "like a church bell on Sunday morning."

"I like it," he replied, "and I can see by the look on your face that you like it too. I've been ringing this bell every Sunday now for almost twenty years. I love to hear the bell sound out the call to worship across the fields. When they retired me from teaching at the high school, I told the session I'd mind the church, sweep and dust, and build the fires in winter, just so I could continue to ring the bell."

"Twenty years is a long time," I ventured.

"Yes, that it is." He scratched his chin thoughtfully. "Many children have grown up around here under the sound of that bell, and many of the elders have gone the long way home as it tolled away the number of their years."

"The bell rings them in and rings them out," I suggested.

"I've thought of that, you know. Somebody could write about life in terms of bells," he observed. "In these days of horns and whistles, the part bells have had in the history of man chances to be forgotten—though many churches lately are installing chimes and carillons again."

He went on, but my mind began to follow his suggestion. "Life in terms of bells." When the baby comes, its first toy is often a cluster of tinkling silver bells; for the youth there are the bells at Christmas time, the sleigh bells in the snow; the minor key of the school bell sounding across the country-side hastens the children's lagging, unwilling feet; the clapping of the happy dinner bell calls workers in from the fields at noon.

"In terms of bells." Wedding bells and the "world of happiness their harmony foretells." "The jangling and the wrangling" of the bells on the wheeling, reeling fire wagon as it rolls thumpingly by. The Sanctus bell calling the faithful out of warm beds to morning prayers. The curfew bell sounding in lonesome tones the "knell of parting day."

In terms of bells! The devoutest prayer of the Englishman for his son, wrote Mr. Ruskin, is that he may be entitled, when visiting a two-belled house, to ring at the visitor's bell, and not at the servant's; and that when he is old, he may himself be able to own a two-belled house. We Americans might seem to covet a two-telephone-belled house, with extension jacks in every room.

In terms of bells. "The throbbing and the sobbing of the bells, the rolling, and the tolling of the bells," at the final hour. Slowly then the bell tolls. No need to hurry any longer. Take your eternity now, it says. Leaden steps for the death march. "The moaning and the groaning of the bells." One stroke, like a period, for each year. He counted once. He counts no more. His tongue is silent, his ear closed. Will he never again hear the euphony of the bells? Yes, thought John Bunyan; yes, he will. When Pilgrim crossed the dark river and the celestial ones led him up to the city, the eternal gates swung open in embracing welcome, and "the trumpets did blow, and all the bells of the city did ring for joy."

"In Lincoln, England, where my people came from—" I aroused from my reverie to find my sexton friend still talking. "In Lincoln, England, I've heard my great aunt say there is a bell, dating from 1604, that has an inscription on it:

> I sweetly toiling men do call
> To taste on meats that feed the soule.

I think of that every Sunday when I pull this bell rope. I'm calling men away from toil to feed their souls on the bread of life."

I was off again after this new quarry of thought, leaving him holding the rope waiting to ring the second bell. Like an inspiration the text of the bell fell into place, and I began to think of it in Paul's triune pattern. The world was still in famine, not a hunger for bread or a thirst for water, but a hunger for the food of faith, hope, and love.

"Meats that feed the soule." Man shall not live by meat, bread, and potatoes only. He must have the inner nourishment of faith—faith in man and faith in God.

Man must have faith in man. The depression at the beginning of the second quarter of our century brought the world a heavy lesson in how literally true this is. There were bread lines in America; millions of our people were going hungry. Not because there was a lack of food. The granaries were stocked. Shelves of our stores were heavy with food to eat and raiment to wear. The cause of the depression was a lack of faith in man. In one day men's hearts failed them for fear and for want of faith. It was the same world as before, just as much money, just as much food, just as many people wanting, but not as much faith in man now. The starving souls brought literally starving bodies. Man no longer believed in man. Suddenly the people discovered that prosperity depended on how the soul prospered. Man had plenty of everything but faith in his fellows. He learned that the most valuable possession of a nation was not giant industries; not Fort Knox caves, bricked with gold ingots; not granaries choked with wheat and corn; but faith, faith in people. The need was not physical but spiritual.

Today the lesson has a more cosmic complexion. Strange in the vision of heaven it must be to see us paying out thousands of dollars every hour for storage on wheat, to see a billion pounds of butter stacked in rancid piles and millions of people starving for bread and butter. The cause? Not enough faith in man. Tonight a million people will sleep on the streets of Calcutta without shelter, lying down after having had but one meal during the day and not such a meal as loads our tables three times a day. And our storehouses glutted with provisions. The hearts of men are so crowded with fear and hate there is no room for faith.

"I have meat to eat that ye know not of." He had that food which came down from heaven, "that a man may eat thereof, and not die" (John 6:50). Men need the food of faith in God. The cynic is only crying out from his hungry soul. The atheist is already dead. He but walks the world, a ghost of what he might be. It is the hunger for God men need to satisfy. God is the author of the hunger, and the answer. When man cuts himself off from the Eternal, he destroys himself.

In Southey's poem "The Inchcape Rock" there is an illustration of this.

The holy Abbot of Aberbrothok
Had placed that bell on the Inchcape Rock;
On a buoy in the storm it floated and swung,
And over the waves a warning rung.

When the rock was hid by the surge's swell,
The mariners heard the warning bell;
And then they knew the perilous Rock,
And blessed the Abbot of Aberbrothok.

Sir Ralph the Rover was a wicked varlet and hated men who talked of God; so one spring day he had his minions row him over to the rock, and he cut down the bell. It sank with a gurgling sound. The Rover laughed:

> The next who comes to the Rock
> Will not bless the Abbot of Aberbrothok.

He turned out to be a prophet who fulfilled his own prophecy. Sir Ralph the Rover scoured the seas for many a day and plundered the vessels he pirated. Then he sailed back to Scotland. His ship, sailing heavy with booty, was dashed on Inchcape Rock. Instead of blessing the Abbot, he cursed himself and drowned.

Come, the bell invites, partake of the soul-living bread of hope. "Life is more than meat," it warns. How starved a fat-fed world can be; how lean obesity! "What is hope?" asks Carlyle, and seemingly without any, he replies:

> A smiling rainbow
> Children follow through the wet;
> 'Tis not here, still yonder, yonder:
> Never urchin found it yet.

If that were true, why live? "While there is life, there is hope." Here the world is longing for the bread of hope, and he has nothing to offer but a scorpion of death. How much more satisfying are the words of Tennyson, "I hope to see my Pilot face to face." Indeed, as the man of Tarsus wrote, "We are saved by hope."

Dan Bryan, long-time conductor on the train that was commonly referred to as "Bryan's Train," said one trip he came to Professor Erb for his ticket. The man searched frantically in all his pockets but failed to find it. Dan assured the professor that it was all right. He could give it to him another time. But the frustrated man replied, "It may be all right with you, Dan, but I've got to have that ticket to know where I'm going."

Man must have the transportation of hope. He must be going somewhere. Surely, if there were no hope, it would be necessary to invent it. All the food in the world will not sustain the soul that has no hope. Man must have strength within to withstand the pressures of life without, or he will be crushed. Edna St. Vincent Millay wrote:

> The heart can push the sea and land
> Farther away on either hand;
> The soul can split the sky in two,
> And let the face of God shine through.
> But East and West will pinch the heart
> That can not keep them pushed apart;
> And he whose soul is flat—the sky
> Will cave in on him by and by.[1]

Men also starve for the bread of love. Bread without love is bitter. Even the small taste of the morsel of understanding is soul strengthening. I called the denominational head-quarters in the city and gave the operator the number; there was considerable delay. The girl seemed to be perturbed, as though she were working under pressure, and so I volunteered, "Take your time, Miss. I can wait." With her voice relieved of its tension, she replied, "Thanks, Mister. That's

[1] From *Renascence and Other Poems.* Harper & Bros. Copyright 1912, 1940, by Edna St. Vincent Millay. Used by permission of Brandt & Brandt.

the first kind word I've heard today." How starved are hearts for the smallest of kindnesses! To them it is the bread of life. I must give out more of kindness, for in giving it to others, I feel my own hunger is fed.

The wise man asserts, "Better is a dinner of herbs where love is" (Proverbs 15:17). No home can be fed and cared for properly, however luxurious it is, however appetizing the meals, if the bread of love is wanting. Better a cottage, better a mess of greens, where there is love.

Ralph Morrell had a good income and one of the finest places in town. He came home one day to find his wife dressed and her bags packed, ready to leave. This was strange; this he could not understand. Here was a beautiful house in which to live, plenty to eat, and the best of fine clothes. When he reminded her of these, she replied, "I'd be glad to trade my fur coat, my best dresses, and all my share in this place, just for love." He had been so busy making money to make a fine home that he had lost it. There is no home, however beautiful, but becomes ugly unless love lives there. How true it is that "hearts starve as well as bodies"!

In the world there is plenty of food for all. How like a paradise it could be if we began to give to others the soul-sustaining food of faith, hope, and love! Ring out, Sabbath bell; call your message to the starving world to come and "taste on meats that feed the soule."

The sexton was ringing the second bell. I was back in my room all ready to go. I had been changing my sermon from "The Ethical Implications of Worship" to "Meats That Feed the Soul."

"Good message you gave," Bruce said after the service. "It rang the bell."

2

A CANDLE FOR THE DARK

I HAVE A CLOSED MIND—ABOUT ANGELS, THAT IS. SUNDAY afternoon Jeb and Whit Paine were arguing about angels. Whit, it seems, also has a closed mind about angels. He was set that there were no such creatures, certainly not as many as ten thousand dancing on the point of a needle. Jeb was not so sure. He is never dogmatic, always leaves the door open and the welcome mat out for new ideas.

But about angels, my mind is made up. I am not completely sure about the feathered kind. I have never seen that variety nor read that Mr. Audubon has ever classified such. Nor have I in my peregrinations through the fields ever picked up a celestial feather wafted down from an angel in its flight. I do admit, as Whit said, that I would be surprised to find a feather of angel size. Still, I've been surprised too many times by things created to be absolutely certain that there are no such celestial creatures that fly as doves from their windows. God would not be unable to do a seraph or cherub, even a million or more. The fact that I have not seen them does not mean there are no angels. I am convinced, however, that it takes more than ten-foot feathers to make an angel. The angel I knew was completely featherless. In fact, as far as looks went, she was no angel at all, but when it came to soul beauty—and what good is angel's plumage if it covers a Belial heart?—I would venture her against any heaven-made, feathered kind of saint.

I see I've given away this angel's gender. When I come to think of it, I read about male angels, like Gabriel, and nothing at all about female angels. Yet every artist paints only lady angels. I suppose most artists, being male, know themselves too well to venture the masculine kind. Anyway, an angel with a beard would look ridiculous.

This angel was Aunt Emma. She is gone now but still of angel memory. Everyone called her "Aunt Emmy"; she was a down-to-earth kind.

Now, angels are where you find them. They are not generally on dress parade. "Stir a clod and start a wing." If one went out looking for wings, one would likely never find an angel. He would just as likely find one in denim or sackcloth. Not that angels are ugly, but they don't always look like heavenly beings, and I believe we have scripture for that. Many have entertained angels unaware. This has its good points, for if the doorbell rang and you went to the door and found an angel standing there, all feathered out, it might be somewhat disconcerting. There doesn't seem to be any book out on how to entertain angels aware, or unaware.

I am not one to say that we ought to entertain every kind that comes to our door; for we can also entertain devils unaware. Of course, there may be some poor devils that need succor quite as much as angels, for it is supposed that angels have everything. One can't waste time waiting for an investigating committee to check the records. It is not too uncommon for ministers of the devil to appear as angels of light. They seem to be clever devils. Of course, the smart wolf would be the one who came just as he was and tried to convince people that he was a lamb in wolf's clothing. So the imp might come the way he is, be the devil he is, and then laughingly confess that he does look like the very devil but that he really is from heaven.

Dan Waters tells about a tramp that appeared at his door and asked for a largess. Now, Dan seems to pride himself that he can see more through a keyhole than most of us can discover through an open door. He refused the beggar's request. When his visitor reminded him of the scripture that he should not be forgetful to entertain strangers for in so doing many had entertained angels unaware, Dan came right out and threw it in his teeth: "I'm sure," he said, "that when angels come to my door, they will not be chewing a quid of tobacco."

So, I'm not recommending that we go wholesale and receive all callers as angels. It is not the devils I am thinking about so much. Judgment belongs to the Eternal. We might be encouraging angels in slothfulness; they might end up becoming lazy devils.

If not by looks or by garb, how are we going to know? Likely not by a letter of announcement, like when the bishop comes, preceded by a neat embossed card sent out from his office. Perhaps not by asking right out, "Are you angel or devil?" If it were an angel, he would likely be too modest to admit it. If a devil, he would not bow and disclose his horns; he would not speak right out and say, "I am Mephistopheles."

As I mentioned, angels are where you find them. After

they are gone, it may come to us, as it did to Abram on the plains of Mamre, that those were surely angels. So it was with Aunt Emma. It was after she had gone and all the neighbors gathered at her funeral that all agreed with Martha Evans, "Aunt Emmy was one of God's angels come to earth."

With that I also agreed. I preached her funeral sermon. I used for my text a favorite saying I had heard her use many times: "If you go looking for the dark with a candle, you'll never find it." So it was, as I said then, she dwelt always in the light, and I maintain still that those who walk in the light are God's angels. It is one sure way of recognizing them.

I used as a scripture text, "The spirit of man is the candle of the Lord." Of woman also, for "Aunt Emmy" was the candle of the Lord.

Uncle Billy Wells was a well-loved lay preacher. He had a parable he used to give about the Creation. The way Uncle Billy described it was that when God resolved to make man, the archangel, arrayed in his badge of celestial office, waited upon the Creator, and importuned that man be made to look like him. The seraphim sent a delegation petitioning that God make man a seraph. The cherubim also sent a committee suggesting that man be made a cherub. But God just made man a human being, "a little lower than the angels." Uncle Billy thought a little lower in looks, in splendor, but certainly not in worth. For, as he would say, there never was a man who would want to change from being a plain human being, to become the finest feathered angel. He always said—and some thought him irreverent—he wouldn't trade one good man for half a dozen cherubs. So God walks about the world with man for his candle. "Ye are the light of the world."

Here are some of the points used at Aunt Emma's funeral: First, the candle burns not for itself but for "all that are in the house" of the world. It gives light only as it consumes itself. Aunt Emma did just that. She lived not for herself. She burned herself out for others. Of course, if you carry a light for others, you'll never walk in the dark yourself. The light that shines for others also lights the way for self, more and more "unto the perfect day."

Secondly, Aunt Emma always looked at the dark with the light. In the light of the things that were good, beautiful, and true. Accordingly she never seemed to discover any dark things about other people. In her light the dark things seemed to fade away. She had the ability to find out and to bring out the best in people. Even in those who seemed to be the worst she had the knack of discovering the good. If that isn't the sign of an angel, then it ought to be. If anyone posed as an angel and always had the devilish trait of pointing out the ugly in others, it seems to me that would be a definite sign that this was a demon only appearing as an angel of light, and that his light was darkness.

And as the last point, darkness flies before the light. The light shines and all the darkness in the world is not sufficient to put it out. Instead of complaining of how dark things were in any given situation, Aunt Emma lighted a candle, and things always took on a better look. Certainly those who look for the dark with the dark will always find it; they even start with the darkness in their own hearts. In every dark situation, when others complained how dark things looked, things always looked brighter when Aunt Emma came in.

At the funeral sermon, I addressed Jonathan Stilley. "You remember, Jonathan, when the yellow telegram came telling you that your son Timothy was killed in action, how dark the day was for you. I came and tried to cheer you, and give you words of encouragement. It was then Aunt Emma came in and quietly said, 'Now, Jonathan, if you go looking for the dark with a candle, you'll never find it.'

"You recall, Sam Lindley, when your wife died and left you with three small children to care for, how miserably you were engrossed in darkness. And most of us sitting there with you nodded our heads gloomily that it was a day of clouds and thick darkness for you. Then Aunt Emma came in like the candle of the Lord. 'If you go looking for the dark with a candle, you'll never find it.'"

"You, Frank, recall when on the church board meeting nights we faced up to insufficient budgets, fuel bills not paid for months, leaks in the roof, and everything looking dark and discouraging; after we had all spoken on the side of our deficits and were sighing in the gloom of things, it happened. It seems that Aunt Emma would take delight in letting it get just as dark as it could, then when we were all enswathed in gloom, she would light her candle of hope. 'If you go looking for the dark with a candle, you'll never find it.'

"And," I continued, as we gathered to do her honor, "we all find out now that we have been entertaining an angel of God, an angel of the light. Wherever she is, she is still God's candle."

3

YES AND NO

It was easy to see that Brother Scarborough was considerably exercised about the way things had gone at the meeting. He had made several speeches for the plan, but it had not carried. He had counted on Deacon Beddenoe to support it, but the deacon had not taken any stand either for or against. Deacon Beddenoe had considerable influence. Had he spoken for the proposition, it would probably have carried. Indeed, Brother Scarborough was certain it had failed because he had remained silent. "Deacon Beddenoe," Brother Scarborough had said in a final desperate bid for his support, "what are your sentiments? Isn't this a good plan, and shouldn't it carry?"

"Well, yes and no, if you know what I mean," was all the deacon had replied.

After the meeting someone remarked that Deacon Beddenoe seemed to be quite lukewarm on the project.

"Deacon Beddenoe," said Brother Scarborough bitterly, "should be called Deacon Yes-and-No. His religion consists in worshiping the god of hems and haws. Too bad he wasn't born twins so that one of him could say 'yes' and the other 'no.' "

"Well, yes and no, if you know what I mean." And

generally people do know. They recognize the maundering attitude that refuses to take any position.

This may stem from a native timorousness. Many people are not able to stand for anything because of the polio of timidity. Brother Scarborough, clever at phrase making, once said, "You may say that silence is golden, but sometimes it is just plain 'yellow.'" It is fear that often makes people betray the innocent and crucify the messiahs.

"Yes and no, if you know what I mean." This answer may issue from the fact that the person is incapable of considering the many modifying factors and of arriving at any certain conclusion. His reasoning powers are lame. He remains noncommittal because he hasn't the qualities it takes to think through and come to any final judgment. How can one express an opinion if he has none? Such a one might more be pitied than condemned. Who could criticize a blind man for not seeing? People may seem incompetent because they are.

"Well, yes and no." Some may flatter themselves that this is the best answer. They think it is smart to "play it safe," to lend their ears to everyone and give their tongue to no one. They imagine that if they stand for nothing, they will not fall for anything. No one has to repent for what he did not say. He will never have to reap what he has not planted.

Jeb tells about stopping one summer day at Lige Plunket's. Lige was happily "bankrupt of life, yet prodigal of ease." When he worried, he went to sleep. His farm and buildings were a commentary on his lethargy. Lige was barefoot and lounged in a barrel-stave hammock.

"How's your corn, Lige?" asked Jeb.

"Ain't got none," he drawled. "Didn't plant any."

"Why not?"

"Afeerd of the cornborer."

"How's your potatoes?"

"Never planted any. Knowed the bugs'd get 'em anyways."

"How's your wheat?"

"Didn't sow none. Feared be no rain."

"What did you plant?"

"Nothin'. I just played it safe."

Others may just say "yes and no" because they are truly wise with a worldly wisdom. They are adroit; their wisdom is on the side of expediency. It might better be termed cleverness. They make their position serve to their advantage. They are crafty in the technique of control. They reserve their opinion until they see which way the majority will go; or they wait until the evidence is all in. This last seems beside the point, since "Mr. Yes-and-No" never arrives at an opinion, at least never expresses partisanship for either side. If he is adroit, it is in acrobatically balancing himself on the fence, courting the favor of both parties and wishing a boon on both houses. He may be Machiavellian in spirit, attempting to divide and rule. In how many instances, indeed, is the chairman chosen because he is neutral and "splendidly null!" Accordingly he may not be stupid but appear to be so by design.

"Mr. Yes-and-No" may be manifesting the better part of wisdom, valor in discretion. Sometimes the answer is "yes and no." Hardly anything is all "yes" and no "no," or all "no" with no "yes." Most often things are "both-and." Few things have been completely decided; or if settled on one day or at one place, they might be unsettled the next time, or at another place. A great many things have to be qualified. Most events are relative. We have to live with partial knowledge. News is coming in all the time about almost everything. Water runs downhill; that seems definite enough. But the answer is yes and no, if you know what I mean. "Yes" if you refer to a stream; "no" if you refer to a faucet up on the tenth floor.

Sometimes it requires quite a little perspicacity to recognize two or more complexions to things. The Greeks were celebrators of the golden mean, the middle-of-the-road position. Someone has quipped that the best man is the meanest man, the one who stays "mostest" on the mean. It does require something of character to maintain balance when everyone else has fallen over to one side or the other. If one does take his stand for something, he has to take his stand at once against something, so that every "pro" is also the manifestation of a "con." If one identifies himself as in favor of this, he is against that.

"Well, yes and no, if you know what I mean." Certainly there are times when it takes fortitude to be neutral. If one declares himself, he at once has the assurance of support from all on his side of the question; whereas if he refuses to pass judgment, he is attacked from both sides. He is caught between; he has to stand alone. He has double the number of enemies and no allies. He is assailed as weak, a "pussyfooter," and a "mugwump." He would be safer if he took his position with others; then he would have some support. But he refuses "to make his judgment blind."

Certainly if he reserves his opinion, even when his mind is made up, he is in a better position to win those with whom he might disagree over to his side. Nothing snaps opposing minds shut more quickly, more tightly, than for one to make snap judgment. And nothing hardens and crystallizes opinions more rigidly than to make an attack from a frontal position. The wise man may have his mind all made up and find that if he reveals his judgment, he has at that point created enough opposition to defeat his proposition. If he is wise enough to reserve his opinion; if he even uses the guile spoken of by the Tarsus apostle, not only to cover up his own conviction in the matter, but to appear even to take the opposite position from what he stands for; he may have a good chance to win through. The oblique attack, even retreat, may win where direct action would fail.

The Reverend Hugh Smart did not belie his name. He had set his heart on erecting a granite cross in the church-yard in memory of the servicemen of his parish who had lost their lives in the war. At the meeting of the session, he hinted that a war memorial would be a nice gesture but that it was too late to do anything about it now. There was an immediate objection, "What do you mean, too late?" He deferred graciously and suggested one inside the church. "Inside the church?" questioned one. "It'd never be seen inside the church." He concurred meekly and thought that a nice varnished board on the outside wall might be nice. "Wood?" protested another. "It'll have to be something permanent, like stone." "Not a cross, of course," the minister thought. "A cross, of course, the very thing." It was unanimously voted to erect a stone cross in the churchyard as a war memorial. After the board meeting the Reverend Hugh Smart called a number by telephone: "You may proceed with the memorial cross I ordered from you last week."

"Yes and no, if you know what I mean." And quite often we know it means the gentler spirit, the spirit of tolerance. Surrounded as we are by intolerance, it is sometimes refreshing to meet a "Mr. Yes-and-No." Modern minds are too brittle, glass-housed minds, that continue to hurl contumelious bricks about. Always feeling that if we could kill off some people who hold an idea in opposition to ours, we could destroy the idea. The truly tolerant mind establishes a difference between the person and the opinion that person may hold. We too often judge the whole person by one conviction he expresses. We forget that every man is a bundle of ideas. It is unwise to damn the whole person because we disagree with one of his opinions. He may hold a score of others with which we are in complete agreement.

The tolerance that is attractive is the one that accepts the whole man. Almost every apple has a spot; in any case we do not eat the core. Parts of even the best things often have to be rejected. It is a mark of maturity to endeavor to like the man even when we disagree with one or more of his beliefs. Quite often apart from our opinions we are very worth while to know. Sometimes the worst thing about a man is his religion. The tolerant man finds the agreeable qualities, emphasizes them, and while there may not be any unity of minds on a proposition or two, there is a unity of spirit. Personality is of more importance than opinion. The letter kills; the spirit gives life.

"Well, yes and no." We have learned that often this seemingly tolerant attitude may be born of mental laziness.

One refuses to take the pains to be informed. Many minds are broad because they are shallow.

Again, such neutrality may be the result of apathy and unconcern. Tolerance that comes from indifference is without virtue. The unreligious man easily proclaims friendship for all because he has no interest in religion. For him there is neither Jew, Greek or Roman Catholic, nor Protestant; he doesn't care because he has no interest.

"Yes and no, if you know what I mean." Often we know that it means a mind without conviction, a personality without direction, a character that stands for nothing and falls for everything. The world has a right to expect that a man stand for something, and is not like a vagabond piece of paper tossed about by every wind of doctrine. If the closed mind allows nothing to come in, neither does the open mind allow anything to stay. Often the open mind is nothing but a hole in the head where everything blows right through.

Some things can be known. They are no longer debatable. There are occasions when one can no longer be a "Deacon Yes-and-No." There is a time for open minds to close. Compromise is no longer possible.

Josh Stump decided to go to New York as a dock worker. Josh had only recently joined the church, and Elder McMinn told him that the dock workers were pretty rough; many of them were blasphemers and irreligious; Josh would have to be careful. Josh went and worked during the summer and came back when the winter set in. He said he had had no trouble at all. He was up there for six months, and not a soul even suspected that he was a church member.

One must not be so anxious to be agreeable that he betrays the right. Even silence can be most articulate in what it does not say. To say nothing, at times, tells everything.

Harmlessness may have some value, but truth is not harmless. Love is not harmless. Men have learned that there are things worse than impatience, than anger, than war. Nature has made up her mind about gravity. One cannot be open-minded about that without breaking his neck. Nature does not try to be kind about its laws. They are inexorable. They are not yes-and-no. They are yes or no; and very definitely so, uniformly and predictably so.

Some things a man must take a position on, hold unqualifiedly to "yes," or adamantly to "no." One cannot be tolerant about communicable disease, about the multiplication table, or about the fidelity of his wife. About some things one must have an unconsenting conscience; they are no longer debatable. Long experience in living has proved and tested them.

"Mr. Yes-and-No" can be entirely reprehensible, guilty of positive evil even though he takes a negative or neutral stand. The Klan was very strong in some areas in the twenties. Many of the leading citizens were members. "Hood-riders," Jeb called them. Bill Atwell was active in the Klan until one night they were in the process of lynching a Negro who was accused but had not been proved guilty. He watched the poor wretched fellow as they bound him to the stake; he with one other was given a lighted fagot to set the blaze. As he advanced, the sense of shame and of justice flared instead. He threw back his hood, tore off the regalia, and resolutely mounted the pyre, and the man within him cried out an unqualified "no."

"I must stand for justice," he cried, "for fair trial. You,

John Drake, you're a deacon of our church. You, Tom Mc-Call, you are the sheriff. Light the wood if you choose. I'll burn with this Negro, but I will not surrender to injustice." It was like a clarion calling all the men back to their senses.

"Well, yes and no, if you know what I mean." You may mean nothing, nothing positively, but how much, Mr. Yes-and-No, you disclose about yourself!

4

"SHOCKINGS ALIVE!"

"Shockings!" say that within Frankfort township, anywhere, and almost everyone who hears will remember "Uncle Jim," even though he has been gone these thirty years. Everyone called him "Uncle Jim," even his own brothers. "Uncle" was a familiar term used by people in this section as a symbol of honor and respect. There were "Uncle Hen Hayes," "Uncle Billy Martin," "Uncle Dode Jones." It was the way the common people elevated those they venerated to their roundtable of knightly living. "I dub thee, 'Uncle.' "

"Shockings!" It was a verbal signal that Uncle Jim had something to say, something he thought was worth hearing. Most people use initial verbal monitors, words like "Say!" "Listen!" "Believe me!" "I'm telling you!" and the like. They are used as heralds to announce entrance upon conversation.

When Uncle Jim thought what he was about to say was something of especial importance, he added a booster, "Shockings alive!" That was the way he said it the morning he was "robbing the bees." There he stood like a blue-denim giant among the tiny white houses in the village of the bees. He had the roof off one little square house, his hand delved deep and his arm aseethe with crawling, yellow dynamite. I stood back on the porch in the circumference of safety.

"Aren't you afraid? Don't you ever get stung?"

"Sometimes; yep, sometimes."

"How do you dare? Bees are dangerous."

"Shockings alive, m'son, if you want the honey, you've got to put up with the bees."

There seemed something of an axiom about that, something that reached out beyond the little colony of the apiary and its product.

Now, most people are fond of honey. "What is sweeter than honey?" asked the Philistines. Perhaps many things are; people differ. Ab Nygren maintained that honey always gave him a sour stomach, while his wife, Effie, said it was the best thing in the world for her throat. But using the word "honey" in a generic way, people might list many of life's honeyed things, things that to them are sweeter than the honeycomb: a happy home; recognition; some position in church, club, or lodge; a political office; money and the things it can purchase. In securing any of these things, the axiom of Uncle Jim's seems to apply. "Shockings alive, m'son, if you want the honey, you've got to put up with the bees."

I take it that everyone wants the honey that is sweet to him. In our kind of world the bees are in business both at the production end and at the protection end, and while we may not like their arsenal of defense, they cannot very well be dispensed with.

If anyone is out trying to find the golden sweetness in the world, he must first locate the bees. Vern Mason knew how to locate a bee tree. There is a definite technique. He took me out with him. I was quite cynical about coming back with anything and would have settled for a quart or less, but Vern insisted that we take along two pails, deep enough to hold about twenty pounds. I carried the two pails swung on the ax handle over my shoulder, and followed with enough doubt to do Thomas and his whole family. Vern went ahead into the wood lot, carrying the bee box with its lure of melted sugar. We came upon a goldenrod cluster, and there were the bees swarming about like a buzzing convention. Vern snapped a bee into the trap and waited. The bee must get a load of the liquid sugar that was in the box. He then opened the box lid. The bee was still busy loading up; soon it heavily arose and lifted itself high to get its bearings, then took the beeline for its home. Vern ran after the bee as far as he was able to see. Then he sat. He assured me that the little fellow would be back. I had no such confidence. But he was speaking with experience; I was hearing with doubt. Soon the little honey maker was back; and not alone. This time it had company; this supply source was too good to keep secret.

John Burroughs describes what happens here in *Pepacton*. When the fortunate discoverer returns to her hive, of course she has the evidence on her feet—shoes all covered with miry, sticky floral sorghum; and gossips about the hive begin to talk: "Oh, did you see that? Peggy Mel came in a few moments ago in great haste, and one of the upstairs packers says she was loaded till she groaned with apple-blossom honey, in October! Fee, fi, fo, fum, I smell something. Let's after!"

Soon Vern, by stages of snare and follow, located the

bee tree, and we did fill the two pails with apple-blossom honey in October. Where the bees are, there also is the honey. As Vern pointed out, if you are out to get honey, first locate the bees.

"If you want the honey, you've got to put up with the bees." The second corollary about this seems to be, if you want the sweet things of life, you've got to run the risk of getting stung. As I mentioned, there are the production end and the protection end. One might object to the protection business end of the bee and decide to eliminate the stings and arrows, but that would kill the bee that makes the golden honey.

There was considerable disturbance and pressure until the king of the beasts had to call a council to deal with the bee problem. The motion was made and seconded to deport all honeybees. Several long speeches were made in favor of the motion. The bees would have to go because their stings were definitely a menace in the U.S.A., United Society of Animals. Bees were dangerous because they carried concealed weapons. Bees should be outlawed because their daggers were not only sharp but also poisonous. Bees would have to be banished because they interfered with animal liberty; everyone had the right to eat his honey in peace. After all had spoken and it looked as if the motion were sure to pass, a bee, whose name the clerk never did get, but a few said he was referred to as "Uncle Jim," droned, "If you want the honey, you've got to put up with the bees."

It is the way the world is planned. All the desirable things have their price. There must be dangers faced and dares taken. Columbus, the discoverers, the pilgrims and pioneers, faced the dragons of risk.

Now, not all the pilgrims and the pioneers returned. Strangely, many had been living in the land flowing with milk and honey and did not recognize it. Sometimes what they had in their own back yard was golden honey, but they sold out and went looking in the farthest pastures of the world. They spent a whole lifetime wandering about like wayfarers seeking and never finding, while there was a bee tree growing in the place they had forsaken.

Many patriarchs did not return but spent their lives in the search. They went out looking for the Promised Land and were lost. They died without having received the promise but having seen it afar off. They did succeed in blazing the trails for others to follow. The world profited by their journeys into the wilderness. They wore out their days believing in it, and while they died, they kept the dream awake. Others who followed them were able to give eyes to their vision, to make their dreams come true.

Many of the sojourners found the land of honey and did not return. They perished because of the stings of the protecting bees. Any commentary needed on this may be found —at least one chapter—in the book of holy martyrs. They were imprisoned, stoned to death, sawed asunder, burned at the stake, and crucified. They met the stings of outrageous misfortune. Many of them died willingly that we might live in the sweetness of life, liberty, and the pursuit of happiness.

Keep in mind, then, this second corollary. If yourself expect life's nectar, you will have to chance the dangers of the stingers in the world. It will mean that you must venture self-denial, hard work, long hours, fatigue, hunger, pain, and all the venomous hornets of discouragement.

You cannot quit just because you get stung. Wherever there are bees, there is the honey, but they will not bring it in and pour it on your griddle cakes.

"If you want the honey, you've got to put up with the bees." But take a warning. All that looks like honey is not made by bees. It may look like honey; but once you have it, alas, it has you. The fly buzzing with delight is convinced he has found the land that is knee-deep in honey; he lands to discover woefully that it is tanglefoot paper. It may taste like honey, be in the mouth sweet as honey, but in the stomach be as bitter as gall. Many are the poor wretches of the world who wish they had never taken the first taste. "Dear is bought the honey that is licked of the thorn"—the thorn that buries itself deeply in the flesh; the thorn of evil habit.

"If you want the honey, you've got to put up with the bees." And Uncle Jim knew how to put up with them. He had the knack of getting the honey without making the bees angry. So many people haven't learned how to get their shares of the sweet things of life without getting others buzzing about their ears. They never seem to be able to get along with people, and they are forever getting hurt, and hurting other people.

Then, there are the timorous, apologetic kind, who always seem to receive the sting rather than the fruit of the bee. Mr. Burroughs says, "They will sting a person who is afraid; they will not sting a person who faces them boldly." There is a certain sadism about people, a cannibalism that seems to make them want to attack the fearful and afraid. The honey seems to belong to the fearless.

"Leave some honey in the hive for the bees to live on,"

warned Uncle Jim. "Dead bees make no honey." I felt that the way he worked, he was taking the honey, not robbing the bees. One must put up the bees, as well as "putting up" with them. All of this is a commentary on unselfish living. Live and help live.

We must learn to get the honey of the world without destroying the hives or killing the bees in our attempts to get it. When Vern found the bee tree, he took the ax and chopped down the tree. The tree was felled, the home of the bees was destroyed, and all the honey was taken. The bees were left to die in the freezing winter. How predatory it all seemed! How like the methods of the nations. War and destruction will not bring the sweetness of world peace.

"If you want the honey, you've got to put up with the bees." We must find ways of getting along with the people in the world. We cannot kill them off just because we get stung now and then. The stingers are the workers. Quite often it is that putting up with the bees that sting is not so difficult as putting up with the drones, the shiftless, and the shirkers. Most of us would be willing to take a sting now and then, particularly if the bee is producing honey.

"Shockings alive!" Uncle Jim, like bees, like people. How very right you were! "If you want the honey, you've got to put up with the bees."

5

THE SERPENT IN THE HOUSE

I HAVE AN IDEA THAT THERE COULD BE SOME REVISION made in the story of those who were invited to come to the feast of good things, when all with one accord began to make excuses. There needs to be a modern version. Something new in excuses has been added.

The new version could still include the old excuse of being too busy. Even though leisure time has been added, things to do have been multiplied.

I went in to see Hart Williams recently—just a friendly call. We had been classmates in school. He hadn't been out to the services lately. Hart had a thriving law practice going. There were several clients in the waiting room. I went up to the secretary and asked if Hart was in. She didn't say; she just asked me a question: "Do you have an appointment?" I felt certain she was not asking for information; she knew that I didn't. I decided not to bother such a busy man, thanked her, and left. As I went away, it occurred to me that even if God wanted to see Hart, he would have to make an appointment with him.

But outside of business responsibilities, almost everyone is out of breath trying to keep up with engagements. People rarely have any time for relaxation. They don't play bridge anymore. They don't play golf. They work at them. I am sure the old version of being too busy to come is still an excuse and is being used more than ever.

In speaking of revising the story, however, the oxen part should be made to fit our 250-horsepower automobile age. For example, one Friday Clayton Arnold telephoned to ask if he could be excused from teaching his class on Sunday: "You see, I've just bought a new convertible, and we are going to take a spin up the river over Sunday."

The excuse "I've just married a wife" might carry a modern version; at least with some people. It might read, "My divorce case is coming up at that very time," or, "I'm leaving for Reno that week end; please have me excused."

The thing that brought to my attention this whole matter of excuse making, and some possible revisions, was my visit with Ward Sidney. His wife has a reserved seat at most of our church meetings, and his two children, Bucky and Clare, are always in church school. So I thought I ought to go over and ask Ward to come along into the church. After the usual amenities, I talked to him about it. I made my invitation as winsome as I could. Then he said, "Well, I never murdered anybody," just as though that settled the whole matter.

Now, this is not something original with Ward. I have heard this excuse used many times, as have all my clergy friends. Because of this much-used, tongue-smooth alibi, I began to think of this as I came away without Ward's consent to unite with the church.

"I never murdered anybody." By this Ward wanted me to think that he was a pretty good fellow, and maybe a little better than some; although I don't think he would be able to point out too many murdering church members.

People keep saying this, "I never murdered anybody," as though this were quite an accomplishment, and as though they should be commended for something. I wonder how much credit ought to be given to the person who never murdered anyone. How much virtue is there in not killing anybody? In not stealing? In not bearing false witness? There were twenty-seven murders committed in my state last year. I didn't do a one of them. How about that? How many stars do I get? Does virtue consist in some evil thing not done? This might work out to a ridiculous end. A rascal might draw his gun and threaten a pedestrian, and then say, "There, I didn't kill you, did I? I'm a pretty good man; I never murdered anybody." He might even demand some reward for not killing: "That will cost you five dollars!" It all sounds ridiculous, but it is something akin to the pitiful logic often used by people. I never murdered anyone; pay me. Some men seem to get such great sums by adding up a column of ciphers: I don't dance; I don't play cards; I don't chew tobacco. Some may even hope to be eternally rewarded for what they have not done.

The example is biblical. A picture is given of one man who read off his account before the Lord: I am no extortioner. I am not unjust. I am not an adulterer. You see, this could go on: "I never murdered anybody."

Now, Ward Sidney might never have murdered anybody because he didn't have a gun; or maybe if he had one, he didn't know how to use it. Perhaps the real reason he had never murdered anyone was that he had never been tempted to. Not many people are. We are not troubled much by the big lions; it is the little foxes that give us the most trouble; not the camels, but the gnats.

Elder Mowbridge had a sermon which he called "The Serpent in the House." It developed from a text in Amos (5:19): "As if a man did flee from a lion, and a bear met him; or went into the house, and . . . a serpent bit him." He said the man had no trouble escaping the lion. It failed to lay a tooth or nail on him. But, pointed out the Elder, the same man went into the house, and a miserable little reptile crawled out of the crack in the wall and nipped him, and he died. When I heard the Elder say that, I said to myself, "I'll venture that was the very man who started this alibi, 'I never murdered anybody.'"

I got away from the lion. Well, what of that? Who doesn't? Indeed, lions are so big one can see them coming a hundred yards away. Besides, lions and bears are scarce; and they mostly inhabit lands far away. Anyway, how many times can a man let a lion bite him and live to boast about it? Nearly everyone escapes the bigger beasts of evil. We get safely home, and while congratulating ourselves, and expecting others to, that we never murdered anybody, we are snagged by a little evil snake, the serpent of evil temper, the viper of sarcasm, the asp of impatience, the adder's tongue of gossip.

People often defend themselves by referring to the relative sizes of sin. One sin is so very big, terrible, and wrong, while their sin is so small. That is a lion. That is a bear. This sin of mine is a tiny worm.

One should remember that the roaring lion was once only a playful whelp, the ugly bear once a roly-poly little cub. Who knows how big this tiny snake might grow to be?

Growth can also be the curse of man. A recent cartoon pictured a man holding in one hand a tiny crocodile and saying, "Isn't he cute?" The second picture showed the beastie had grown, and the man was saying, holding the animal in both arms, "He is quite harmless." The third scene disclosed the man was no longer able to hold the dragon. He stood with his foot on its ugly head and was saying, "I am still master of it." In the final act the leviathan was swallowing down the hapless man, but he was still assuring everyone, "I can get rid of him any time I want to." Let it be kept in mind that the man-eating crocodile was also once only a tiny reptile.

From the standpoint of respect and recognition of worth and manhood, the world is much more ready to applaud the man who fell battling the lion or fighting the bear. Certainly the people have more regard for the man fighting in the lion dens of temptation than the self-righteous who boast that they never murdered anybody, and who pretend that they are not like these publicans, while the little serpents of evil are crawling upon them. How dare we judge the murderer, the thief, the extortioner, when we are rude, impatient, cruel, and without mercy? Don't boast to others about how many lions you have escaped, how many bears could never lay a paw upon you, if you are alive with the creeping little sins.

There is one other point that Elder Mowbridge might have elaborated—it was in the house that the man was bitten. A nursery rhyme has a pig there, but lions and bears rarely get into parlors. In our homes, there the little serpents wait. We can be so gracious and polite to strangers outside, but so impatient, short tempered, and cruel with our own.

Lem, Jeb's hired man, said he never realized how much a voice could change until his wife quit nagging him and answered the telephone.

"I never murdered anybody." No, not with a gun, not with an ax at one blow. But many are slain by the constant venomous stings of little crawling reptiles; the bite of sarcasm, the nip of criticism, the nibble of nagging, the gnawing of faultfinding, the sting of reproach; until love is assassinated; until welcome death comes to release the bolts of torment and set free the prisoner of pain.

You never murdered anybody, but your whole life of action and conduct may be murder incorporated. The foulest crime in our county was committed by a husband outwardly honored and apparently harmless. No one could believe he would murder anybody, but he killed his highly respectable wife by putting small drops of cyanide into her cup of coffee every day. More merciful is murder at one blow than to cause another to die daily.

In the house the little "varments" lie hidden from the eyes of the neighbors because they are cowardly. We are courteous to others because we wouldn't dare be otherwise. At home we take cruel advantage of our loved ones, for there is little they can do about it without exposing our shame and trouble. Marriage ties are so binding; there are children to consider; there is home respect and honor to be thought about. Parents are at the mercy of their children and have to take the stinging, scurrilous things that are "sharper than a serpent's tooth." Children are defenseless against evil-tempered parents. There is nothing they can do because of their utter dependency. The hidden serpents are cowardly, because if we used such abuse against strangers, we would run the risk of having our faces punched.

They are base and hypocritical. We appear to others to be courteous, kindly, and genteel. In the presence of others we are refined and polished, but let us once get into the house, where we are not observed by the public, and we often revert to the liar and cheat we truly are; we become our nasty selves. When one is indeed a person of moral worth and integrity, those who dwell in the house with him will be convinced of it.

In the house of one's own church the little vipers lie. Here the members claim redemption from the evil lions and from the huge grizzlies of wrong. Once inside, they often harbor in their bosoms the miserable little creatures, criticism of the choir, gossip about another member whom they do not understand, shameless remarks about officers of the congregation, carping judgment of the minister. They "bite like a serpent, and sting like an adder."

No, not murder by direction, and let us think perhaps not by intention; things for which we should never be put out of the church; but murder, no less.

So, Mr. Sidney, whoever, wherever, you are with your excuse, "I never murdered anybody," don't be too self-righteous because you have escaped the lions and the bears; watch out for these little vipers. They will kill you. They are murder.

6

HAVE YOU LEFT ANYTHING?

"SUDS IS TIDY, IS SUDS"—THAT'S WHAT HER MOTHER TOLD me the day I took her from her home to a home of her own. "She'll have everything in place and will never leave anything behind." These words I have had cause to remember many times during the happy, hurried years of our life together. Tidy and thoughtful, two graces for happy living.

The first reminder of what her mother had said came on our honeymoon. We had packed the baggage and were ready to leave the hotel room, and there it was—the little warning sign on the door: "Have you left anything behind?"

"Have you left anything behind?" echoed Suds. I was certain we had secured everything. She thought she had better take another look around. The sign was firm with its cold enameled warning. "Suds is neat, is Suds. She never leaves anything behind." Drawers were yanked out to reveal only yawning emptiness: one, two; the dresser, the bureau, the desk. The desk! And there it rolled out—my new fountain pen, a graduation present!

As I have said, a sermon is where you find it, and the minister is always questing. Often sermons are discovered in the humblest places. Jacob had a vision when he used a stone for a pillow. Gideon received a message while he was busy on the threshing floor. Elijah heard the voice of the Eternal under a juniper tree. Jonah found a message in a gourd. Robert Burns thought of one when he discovered a louse. The Nazarene found sermons everywhere—in leaven, in salt, a candle, mustard seed, lilies, the grass of the field, hen and chickens. As the poet has spoken:

> But in the mud and scum of things
> There alway, alway something sings.

From this neat little hotel sign thoughts came to me as from a scripture.

"Have you left anything behind?" There are the inevitable things, things we are compelled to leave behind. Life is a leaving. It is a port from which we are always embarking. As the Book keeps saying, "It came to pass." The world knows little of permanence.

> A mighty monarch in days of old,
> Made offer of high honor wealth and gold,
> To one who would produce in form concise
> A motto for his guidance, terse, yet wise.
> A precept soothing in his hours forlorn,
> Yet one that in his prosperous days would warn.
> Many the maxims sent the king, men say.
> The one he chose, "This too shall pass away."
> O jewel sentence from the mine of truth,
> What riches it contains for age or youth.
> No stately epic measured and sublime
> So counsels or comforts for all time.
> Go write them on your heart
> And make them of your daily life a part.
> Has some misfortune fallen your lot?
> This too shall pass away, absorb the thought.

And wait; your waiting will not be vain.
Time guilds with gold the iron links of pain.
The dark today leads into light tomorrow.
There is no endless joy, no endless sorrow.
Are you upon earth's heights? No cloud in view?
Go read your motto again: This too
Shall pass away; fame, glory, place power,
They are but little baubles of the hour.
The truest greatness lies in being kind,
The truest wisdom in a happy mind.
He who desponds, his Maker's judgment mocks;
The gloomy Christian is a paradox.
Only the sunny soul respects its God.
Since life is short we need to make it broad.
Since life is brief, we need to make it bright.
Then, keep the old king's motto well in sight,
And let its meaning permeate each day;
Whatever comes, this too shall pass away.[1]

Now, this going is necessary that the coming might be. We live in a world where parting is such sweet and bitter sorrow. We long to hold on to many things, yet we would all wisely vote for their going. Who does not love a baby; and who more than its mother? But she does not want it to remain a baby. She wants the baby to go that the child may be, the child to leave for the man to come. A twenty-one-year-old infant would be somebody's heartache. So it is, there are many things we must leave behind. We may grow nostalgic about them, romance about them, sing ballads about them, like "When You and I Were Young, Maggie," "My Old Kentucky Home," but the "gone things were to go." They "came to pass."

[1] Ella Wheeler Wilcox, Poems of Power. Used by permission of Rand McNally & Co.

But life has also its optional things, things we may choose to take with us, and things we may let go of. The responsibility of choice is upon us, and while our closets and attics are cluttered with things we have chosen to keep, the wastebasket is emptied almost every day. Here lies more proof for man's power to choose than half a library of books. That we always make wise choices is undebatable. We don't. No one would want to defend his judgment as infallible. Many things we have thrown away we should now like to have returned to us. If we had to choose over again, we would keep them.

While his wife was away on a visit, Bill Perry decided to buy a new bedroom suite and have it for a surprise for her when she returned. The old bed he sold to a secondhand dealer. When his wife came home, he proudly took her in to show her the new furniture. She was truly surprised and seemed overjoyed. Later Bill was doing the milking, when he heard a shriek, and his wife came running into the barn white as a ghost—scaring the cow and Bill too. Amid tears of frustration she demanded to know what had happened to the mattress. She had been hiding her butter and egg money in it. Bill hurried into town. The old mattress was dug out of the basement of the store and returned to Bill. Mattresses weren't worth anything; nobody wanted to buy a secondhand, worthless mattress. But this one was worth $250.

Salvage companies make millions every year on what other people throw away. Junk dealers have become wealthy. Antique stores are everywhere collecting items from the garrets of old homes. Two of the frailest chairs we have in the house Suds dug out of the debris under the church and had refinished; two little rosebud chairs that cost more to refinish than their price when they were new. No one dares to sit on them, but apparently they are worth quite a lot, according to some people anyway.

Many things we have kept are of little value now. Basements, trunks, and attics attest to this. Anyone who hasn't found out about this will have a surprise coming if he ever has to move. Every minister knows about this. Many of the items we collect are valueless; many reflect our life interests.

"Have you left anything behind" that you should have left? What should we toss out and leave behind that is of no value, that is harmful? All the old harbored grudges that clutter up good living should be thrown into the wastebasket. Some miserable people are all weighted down with the baggage of old enmities that should have been forgotten long ago. Too many people love their hatreds. When you visit with them, it isn't long until they drag them out and display them as Suds does her antique chairs, as though they were something to be cherished.

Brother Tom Heard tells of a feud that he found in his first church. It had been going on for years. Two men wanted the same job. Each felt he was the rightful janitor. One would get up and go to the church and build the fire for the Sunday-morning worship service, and when he went home, the other would go down and put out the fire and build another. Somehow he must have thought it was unholy, like strange fire. One of the janitors sold an asthmatic organ that had been useless for years for ten dollars. The other created such a riot about it in the church that the first had to go and buy it back and return it to the basement, where it sat next to the furnace. When Brother Heard became minister, he had it brought up to the pulpit one Sunday morning and preached a sermon on "Our Beloved Hatreds." Then with an ax he hewed that Agag to pieces before the Lord, and it was used for kindling the fire in the furnace. "Let us throw out of our church this feud," he pleaded. There was a chorus of "Amens." The two janitors were put to shame. Brother Heard had them come to the altar; he offered prayer for them and had them shake hands, and there was rejoicing again in that Israel. Yes, he said, a new janitor was engaged.

"Have you left anything behind?" Let it be affirmed that we have indeed; all of our malice, bitterness, dissensions, evil imaginations, prejudices, and grudges. The flower of goodness cannot flourish in the sour soil of hatred.

"Have you left anything behind?" There are the inadvertant things. There are the unfortunate impressions we did not choose to leave, but nonetheless we have left them. Like a spark falling from a passing train, running on its own right of way, on its own schedule; a fire was set, and while the train goes on, the conflagration scorches the earth behind it. We do leave behind, unintentionally, words and deeds that burn and destroy. And, since all do, let us be forgiving. Mercy is to be offered, and forgiveness. There may be no room for blame, since we are all under the same condemnation.

Tim Hadley always blamed himself. He left the ax behind on the woodpile. His five-year-old son, trying to sharpen a stick, cut off his hand. It was a tragedy. Few people thought unkindly of Tim. How then? The deed done unintentionally, though tragic in its consequences, must not damn the doer. "I will have mercy," saith the Lord, not the sacrifice of the victim that unwillingly did the unfortunate act.

"Have you left anything behind?" There are the words we have spoken. Few are the words spoken in deliberate malice; many are said thoughtlessly. Words spoken were the first to reach supersonic speed—at least they seem to travel faster than sound. And the cruel ones fly away like jets before the good words leave the ground. Once the evil words fly, they cannot again be gathered up.

Father Walsh tells of a monk who was troubled because he had thoughtlessly helped to circulate an untrue story about his friend. He went to his father confessor, who told him, "If you wish to make peace with your conscience, fill a bag with chicken feathers and go to every dooryard in the village and drop one feather." He went and did as he was told and returned to his confessor and announced that he had done penance for his folly. "Not yet," said the prelate. "Now take the bag and gather up all the feathers again."

"But that is impossible," the monk remonstrated. "The wind has blown them all away."

"So," he was told, "words are so easily dropped, but you can never get them back again."

Words and deeds that wound have been left behind. No one of us is without this sin. Since we all have sinned, let us all be merciful to ourselves.

In due consideration, let us recognize that there are good deeds and good words that we should have left behind, but unfortunately we failed. They were waited for, expected. But lives had to go away empty and disappointed. If you are among the disappointed, take hope. If you have failed to leave behind the "helping word," you have discovered that others in the world are fallible as you are. And if now it is too late to mend your omission—someone has now gone the long way home—remember there is no lack of needs and opportunities. There is always a market, a demand for the good deed to be done, for the good word to be said.

"Have you left anything behind" of goodness? No doubt of it. And "there shall never be one lost good!" You may even have forgotten, but the Eternal remembers. "When saw we thee an hungered, . . . sick, . . . in prison?" Well, he replies, you've likely forgotten all about it; I haven't.

"Have you left anything behind" of goodness? Of course we want to; and we hope to. "Do one good deed a day" is a good rule for youngsters. Doing good all day every day is the ideal. We won't make it, and we know that. Certainly the Lord knows that and will deal with us not according to our mistakes but according to his lovingkindness.

"Have you left anything behind?" At funerals it is often asked, "Did he leave anything?" The answer is always, "Yes, he left everything." There comes the day for all, the leaving day, and none escapes. Blessed is he who leaves things behind that are of true worth. Being dead, they still live, move, and have their being; they yet speak. It takes more than death to destroy the good man; and no grave is deep enough to inter virtue.

"Suds is neat, is Suds. She never leaves anything behind." What about that? Ah, many good things she has left; and even a few bad things; which, because of her goodnesses, we have forgotten.

"Have you left anything behind?" Yes, everything; left in thy hands, O Lord.

7

THE ADDED TOUCH

WE WERE ON OUR WAY EARLY ENOUGH. THAT IS ALWAYS a satisfaction. Jeb is like I am; we both like to be on time, maybe a few minutes ahead. The minutes one is ahead of time are never lost; they are added to the life expectancy of the one who has been waiting. The minutes you are late are lost forever; you have squandered them, and those waiting for you have had their lives curtailed by the worry, always a heavy taskmaster.

"Be here at three," Rance had said, "and we'll leave immediately. I'll have the boat all ready, motor in place, and we'll go up the lake to Baptism River; fishin' should be good there if it is anywhere. We'll fish right on through sundown."

Jeb and I were there before three. Rance shuffled out with a dejected look. "We'll have to wait a mite. I let Jake, my hired man, take the boat over to Grandview about one, and he ain't back yet. Said he wanted to get a pair of shoes tapped."

We unloaded and carried our gear down to the small dock. Jeb and I put on our waders and unleashed our lines. Then we waited, and, to make the story short, the waiting was long. Rance paced impatiently. "I told him to be sure and get back early so's I could get the boat ready," he kept repeating.

It was a waiting to no purpose. The hired man did not return. It had been an afternoon wasted for all three of us. Just before I started the car, Rance made a remark that I kept thinking over on our way back home. "You know," he ventured, "if people only did just what they're supposed to do, it'd be a perfect world."

There certainly was plenty of reason for Rance to make such an observation. A great deal of the world's disappointment is caused by the slackers. Most of us are guilty of slackness. Few would dare to cast the accusing stone at others for fear of breaking out their own windows.

"If people only did what they are supposed to do." It certainly would help all right. Much of our negligence is due to absent-mindedness; it may be better to say "crowded-mindedness." Man can shave and never think about shaving. While he dresses, brushes his hair, knots his tie, his mind is running with the hounds of dogging business responsibilities. His mind is absent because the business of the world is too much with him. But if he could get the habit of carefulness, like brushing his teeth, like shaving, his mind could follow the hounds of business, and these neglected things would be cared for automatically and helpfully.

"If people only did just what they're supposed to do." It certainly would help, no question. It is easy to fall into the habit of taking things for granted. We soon learn that others will care for our carelessness. We readily eat up like apples the good things of life without thinking and without showing appreciation.

No wife ever set a better table than Lizzie Vollmar. She

spent long, hot hours preparing a big dinner that was bolted down by Big Jim and the hands in a few minutes; and never any word of appreciation. During haying Big Jim and the workers came in with harvest-hand appetites, and Lizzie brought in a steaming dish of boiled cornstalks. When Big Jim remonstrated, Lizzie quietly said: "I didn't think you ever noticed what I set on the table. You gulp down what I prepare every day and never say a word."

Our carelessness discloses that we take all the comforts of life for granted—clean house, money brought in regularly, laundry done—as if we deserved them. If manna were to fall regularly, we would think it our due every morning. And if one morning it were boiled cornstalks, many would likely cry, "What's the big idea!"

"If people only did just what they're supposed to do." But they don't. Many times it is difficult not to suspect that much of this dereliction is more than mere heedlessness. Sometimes it is easy to feel that it is actually malicious. Some seem to think that it is clever and smart to let the other fellow carry their load, pay their obligations. Predatory living is not uncommon to some people, who treat others as ripe grapes to be skinned and crushed to make jam for their already buttered bread. Probably few such people would admit that they are following the plan of deliberately taking advantage of others, of reaping where they have not sown; but so many are that we have to have laws for protection against such. Go to the store for a box of berries or a bushel of peaches, and you often find proof of predatory merchandising. In any case it is safe to admit that a lot of people are willfully indolent and recreantly negligent.

I had to admit that Rance had a point. If everyone carried

his proper portion of life's load, the sad old world would be a happier place in which to live; and I agreed that it was true that a great number of people were not doing it.

Suds and I made a call on Harvey Scott. He had been in bed with what he called "the miseries." Harvey was a giant of a man but was like a baby and took it easy, most of the time in bed. His wife was a small, worked-out woman. She was always waiting on her husband. When we came away, Suds said it seemed to her that mostly it is the weak who are having to bear with the infirmities of the strong. No question, Rance was more than half right. It would be a big help if everyone did what he is supposed to do.

It was the way Rance said it: "If people only did just what they're supposed to do, it'd be a perfect world." With that way of stating it I had to disagree. The way things are, if everybody only did just what he is supposed to do, the world would be almost ruined. If all did no more than they are supposed to, life would have to come to a standstill. Indeed, if man from the beginning had done the bare minimum of things, the world would still be chaos. A holy discontent with things as they are has brought advancements. Enoch walked with men and found time also to walk with God. Nobody in Ur expected Abram to leave the comforts of home for the uncharted wilderness. Moses ordinarily should have been satisfied to dwell in marble halls, but he chose rather to tabernacle in the desert with the dispossessed. Trained soldiers thought a stripling David foolish to move out against a thundering giant; after all, he had the sheep to look after. Paul must have had enough trouble with the nagging thorn. Why should Columbus risk the leviathans of the unknown, uncharted deep? No one else would. Why do it, Mr. Carey, Dr. Grenfell, Albert Schweitzer? Many of the best people think it is foolish. Men were supposed to ride in ox carts, mold candles, live in log houses, tread the wine press, flail the grain. What else? Weren't these good enough for their fathers?

It is because some burned the midnight oil, arose early in the morning, looked a little longer through the microscope, went out blazing trails, while others dwelt in ceiled houses; because some kept working beyond quitting time, went a little further than the world has come out of its Paleozoic state; because some did more than they were supposed to do, some who had a holy dissatisfaction with the status quo.

And it is because some high-souled people do more than they are expected to do that life keeps going at all. They lift more than their share, carry more than their own weight. They go beyond the second mile, for they realize that it is at the third-mile post that progress begins. They finish what is expected of them and look about to help with the unfinished. They arise early; they not only heed the call of duty but knock on its door before its alarm goes off. They give the added measure to the world's cup of pleasure and refuse to add to its brimming bowl of sorrow.

Jeb has a word for it. He was out for one of Suds's Sunday dinners. He pushed back from the table with a sigh of complete satisfaction. "Suds," he said, "your meat ain't any better'n I always have at home, the baked potatoes no tastier, the salad just common. I've eaten just as good a pie as this many times. But I love to come here because your dinners are the best anywhere around. Know why? It's the added touch—the posy on the table; your hand-painted china, the cherry on the fruit salad, the garnish on the meat, the wedge of cheese on the pie, and a napkin that covers your lap." The added touch! Doing more than is expected.

It is the business that does only what it is supposed to do that oftenest fails. The ones who sell the same kind of goods but give the added touch succeed. The hotel that places the paper at your door in the morning, has the maid turn back your bed in the evening, and extends unexpected courtesies all day long usually is well patronized. Maybe when all do this, some enterprising manager will come up with an extra added touch.

Suds went with me to a convention, and at the hotel where we stayed, there was a box with the invitation, "Please advise us as to how we can give you better service." She dropped in a suggestion. I was a little surprised when I read it. There might have been something of a reaction on her part; it might be an idea. She wrote, "Why not try tipping the guests?"

The restaurant that serves the extra cup, has a flower on the table and a basket of choice rolls, and gives service with a smile; the automobile company that makes a car with extra room, added refinements, and handy devices; the gasoline station with helpful attentions and cleanliness; the builder who makes homes with extra closet space, step-saving kitchens; these have learned the secret of winning favor and business.

In the world of labor-and-capital relations this principle could be happily applied. Friction develops at the point where each does only what it is supposed to do and nothing more. Men come in and go out by the clock. Many spend time watching it. Owners badger the workers to see how much work they can get out of them with how little pay.

Several box factories in our town couldn't make a go of it, but John Morris kept increasing his business. I presume his boxes were no better, but he had no friction in his shop. He knew his workers man by man. When one was absent, John inquired about him. If he was ill, a doctor was sent. Only what he should do, you say? But wait, that was only the beginning. As long as he was ill, John called on him. He not only touched the man when he gave him the job, and again as he met him in the shop and called him by name, and again when he sent the doctor to wait upon him in his need, but he gave the added touch. He went! Others might be hired to keep his books. John kept his men, and his business.

Now, it is no secret that the church that does only what it is supposed to do will not grow. The church that offers the little choice extras wins. The same Bible, the same hymns, the same gospel, but the friendly greeting, the feeling of reverence, the neat bulletin, these attract. The church is blessed that has members who do more than they are expected to do.

Arthur Daniels joined the church when he was eighteen. For several Sabbaths he was so thrilled with his experience that he sat in the first pew. But, feeling neglected, he drifted back pew by pew until in a few months he dropped into the back row. One Sabbath he felt so forgotten that he left before the service had finished and wandered out alone to the buggy shed behind the church. He was on his way out. Then he felt a friendly arm about his shoulder, and a deacon was asking, "What's the matter, Arthur?" It was a small gesture, but Arthur Daniels was saved to become a powerful minister and eventually the elected head of his denomination. He often referred to this added touch.

You see, it doesn't take much—a cherry on the grapefruit, a flower on the table, a small attention. One night at a youth meeting the leader asked the young people to speak on the theme, "What, more than anything else, has kept you for the good way?" Several spoke, but the speech I remember was made by a quiet little girl. She seldom spoke in meeting. She said, "Many times I am tempted to do wrong. But I never can. I always think of my mother. Every night before she goes to bed, she comes and softly opens my door, comes to my pillow, and gently kisses me good night. I pretend that I am asleep, but I know she is there. I cannot get away from the touch of my mother." The added touch!

Don't you see, Rance, why I have to disagree with you? It's the people who do more than they are supposed to do who make life worth living, whom we honor and cherish.

A Carpenter did. He gave the extra touch to the blind, the leper, the publican, the Magdalene. To people whom others would not touch for the first time. He has become the joy of all generations, the fairest of ten thousand, because he went a little further. He gave the added touch.

8

THE BEAUTY OF THE IMPERFECT

We were quite certain when Jeb left for the coast that he meant to stay. He certainly had made such preparation. It was one of the sad days, the day he took the train and I bade him good-by; it was one of the glad days when he returned. He was wearing his Mr. Mona Lisa smile, which disclosed that he was pleased to be back again. After confessing how joyous it was to have him home, I asked, "How was it, Jeb? Didn't you like it?"

He was not a man of effusiveness, but he did seem enthusiastic about the place on the coast. The weather, he said, was perfect; the flowers were perfect; perfect places to live.

"How is it that you didn't want to stay if things were so perfect out there?"

We were approaching Jeb's old place; there was the picket fence with several palings out; there was the chimney that needed repair, the barn wanting a coat of paint.

"Well, I'm glad I went." He gazed rapturously about the old place. "Things were rather perfect out there. Now that I'm back again, for the first time I've come to realize the beauty of the imperfect."

"The beauty of the imperfect." The idea stuck to me

like a Spanish needle. I had always been thinking in the opposite direction—the beauty of the perfect, the attractiveness of the flawless, the completeness of the consummate. Could the imperfect have appeal? Perhaps here was something my mind had missed. Perhaps in beholding a distant rainbow, I had walked over a pot of gold.

When we look about for the perfect, where is it to be found? It is unearthly; it is not of this world. "Neither is it to be found in the land of the living; the depth saith, It is not in me: and the sea saith, It is not with me." All is incomplete. In nothing has the last word been said. Apparently there is nothing that cannot be improved. It is the kind of world in which we live, the kind of world God made. When he finished creation, he did call it good. He did not call it perfect. It was not pronounced complete. And his injunction to the man he made was to "replenish the earth, and subdue it."

Gabe Daily, who liked to pose as an atheist, had arguments as fallacious as any: "Why didn't God, if they is one, make things perfect? Even the sun has its spots. Seems like God could have at least made the planets to run on schedule without us having to add a whole day every four years to make up the time lost. Seems about as bad as Bryan's train."

It is folly to accuse God of being unwise. He made minds; he himself could not be thoughtless. So it must be the best kind of world for our kind of people to live in. There are things to do. Get busy, "replenish the earth, and subdue it." There are bridges to build, oceans to cross, cities to plan, food to raise, schools to be established, mountains to be climbed, and a better world to be created. All about us is the call of the imperfect. The inspiration to be useful; the glory of being of service. The greatest need of man is to be needed. There is no incentive in the perfect.

There is a going-on-ness about the world. We finish only to begin all over again. We build roads only to wear them out. We wash the dishes only to use them over again. We make the beds for the day only to sleep in them when the night comes. Albert Schweitzer told Fulton Oursler:

In a railway station I watch a man with a dustpan and broom sweeping up refuse in the waiting room. He cleans up a portion, then moves on to the next. But let him look back over his shoulder and he will behold a man throwing a cigar stump on the floor, a child scattering paper around—more litter accumulating where a moment before he had it all swept clean. Yet he has to go right on with his work and feel no rage. So must we all! In my personal relations with people I must never be without my pan and broom. I must continually clean up the litter. I must rid myself of dead and useless things. If the leaves do not drop off the trees in autumn, there will be no room for new leaves in the spring.[1]

Make room, says everything; there are improvements coming along. The perfect is not yet.

And in building the world man also builds man; in replenishing it, he replenishes himself. His glory is in the unfinished, and in that glory is his strength. If all were perfect, where would man be? How could he live without living for something?

"The beauty of the imperfect." There is no denying that there is the imperfect that is ugly. Not all imperfect things

[1] *The Reader's Digest*, October, 1949. Used by permission.

are attractive. The misshapen, the blemished, the deformed, the disfigured, are not pleasing. But there is something to do about these things. About the perfect nothing can be done. If it is perfect, nothing can be added to it, nothing taken away from it. It needs nothing. It is an invitation to idleness and decay. Such a situation would be destructive to man— to his happiness first of all.

Uncle Jackson Jones had about as nice a farm as there was anywhere around, and everyone was surprised when he sold out in the fall. Of course, he received a good price for the place, enough to retire on. He said he was glad to get away. The barn needed a new roof. The house had to have a coat of paint. The fences were run down. He moved into town and built what he considered a perfect place. Indeed, when people asked him how he liked his new home, he replied, "Perfect, just perfect." And it did seem to have everything, all the latest gadgets and handy things. He was proud of his place; had a picture of it in the local paper. And Uncle Jack settled down to take life easy. Often when you passed, you could see him on the front porch in his rocking chair. He made trips to the store. Went to the depot to watch the train come in.

When it came spring, it was plain that he was getting restless. During breaking time he went out to the farm— said he just went out to get some fresh eggs. But that one summer was all he could "abide." He bought the old place back, had the house painted, and put a new roof on the barn. "Just couldn't stand it," he explained. "The new house was too perfect. Nothing needed fixing. This is about the happiest day of my lfe—this coming back." I thought of Jeb's coming back home: "For the first time I've come to realize the beauty of the imperfect."

While there are imperfect things that are ugly, the perfect would be more forbidding, where "nothing needed fixing" and where people were "the glass of fashion and the mould of form." The imperfection of perfection lies in that it brings no happiness to man, no permanent joy. Weighed against the true facts of living, it falls short.

Libby Bailey took the prize at the county fair for her perfect pound of butter. It was molded nicely with a neat rose on top. Later she took it to the store in trade for a pound of coffee. When she came home, she carefully weighed the coffee and discovered it was not a pound. She returned the coffee and impolitely informed Mr. Crawford that the coffee didn't weigh a pound. "It must be a pound, Libby," Mr. Crawford informed her. "I used your pound of butter as a weight."

In human relations the beauty of the imperfect seems to work out. The perfect man is marked. The perfect woman is often "nasty nice." Those who think themselves perfect often make their perfection the ugliest thing about them. People seem to be liked most who touch the ground somewhere, who have some redeeming vice. Certainly few are the ones disliked because of their perfection, for every Achilles has his heel.

Quite often the very imperfection itself is the attractive thing. "I think Helen has such a cute stutter," says Alvin. "I just love to hear Elder Warren lisp; it makes his preaching even more attractive," says Clara. So we have the paradox of the perfectly imperfect, the beautiful ugly, to think

about. And we have the surprise of finding the perfect that
is impossible.

There was considerable stir about when Ed Massey left
his home and hired out to work on the Richardson farm.
His wife, Martha, was as spic and span a housekeeper as
there was anywhere. At the divorce proceedings the judge
wanted to know why Ed would walk out of such an excellent place. Ed told the judge, "I just couldn't live with
my wife because she was too perfect."

In talking about this Jeb said he wasn't surprised. He had
seen Ed and his wife one day in the Bon Ton. They had
come in for supper. They had no more than been seated
till Martha began to rearrange the dishes, wipe off the silver-
ware with her napkin, and reset the table. She insisted that
Ed do the same, much to his discomfiture. She helped him
arrange his napkin, told him which spoon to use, not to
make such a noise with his soup. "She's the kind of
woman," suggested Jeb, "that wears herself out getting
ready for company. The guests go away saying that she is
a good housekeeper, but a poor hostess." Some people are
like that. They need another sense of values, to realize the
joys of a home that is lived in, to allow freedom of expression to others, and to cultivate a sense of humor.

"The beauty of the imperfect." We had quite an exercise
in what to do about our organ for the church. It was not
a matter of raising the money; we had that in hand. It was
a question of whether we should buy an electronic organ
or recondition our old pipe organ. I took occasion to talk
with an organist of ability about his opinion. In explaining
the differences in tone quality and in depth and resonance,
he made an interesting observation. "People don't particular-

ly care for the perfect," he said. And there it was. He went on to point out that there were ranks of pipes in an organ that played the same note, not two of them perhaps exactly on pitch. The instrument may be tuned one day and be a little out of tune the very next day because of heat or cold. Even electronic organs are using revolving disks in their speakers so that the sound does not come out so precisely.

"People don't particularly care for the perfect." Here is a great symphony orchestra; maybe there are forty violins, not all of them exactly on pitch, not all fingered perfectly; but people love symphonic music. Here is a band of a hundred or more instruments, harmoniously out of harmony, playing close on to the perfect, but never quite attaining it, and yet thousands are attracted. In the chorus at school the director was warned, "Carol won't do; she sings sharp." "Then I must have her," was the reply, "to balance my flats in the choir." So are the great choruses with many voices, singing only closely around the key, but what beauty of imperfection!

All is approximation. We can take our courage in this. How beautiful are the flowers, so many shapes and colors! Which is perfect? None of them is. Indeed, what is a perfect flower? Who can say? That must be most nearly perfect that pleases most and inspires most. Here are the people, all God's children; so many kinds and colors. Which is perfect? None is. God also must know the beauty of the imperfect.

The Man of Galilee was not perfect in the sense that he needed nothing. He was born of a woman, made under the law. He needed food, sleep, friendship, and love. If we are to take the statement of the prophet as describing him

(Isaiah 53), then he had "no form nor comeliness," and he was not beautiful. God purposed that no physical attraction should detract people from the power of the message he gave. Nor did he ever claim to give the final word about living the good life. He knew what was beyond the comprehensions and capabilities of the people. He would not set before them the perfect that would completely discourage them. "I have yet many things to say unto you, but ye cannot bear them now." There were things to say but no ears keen enough to hear them, no hearts large enough to receive them, no ability great enough in the people to carry them out.

And when that which is perfect is come, be it heaven itself, it will be, in wise providence, a place of beauty. If there is still in man the attractiveness of the imperfect, we shall have to "grow up like calves of the stall," and "they shall build houses, . . . and they shall plant vineyards, and . . . long enjoy the work of their hands" (Isaiah 65:21, 22).

In the meantime look now. Your happiness lies not yonder toward some perfect day; your happiness is here, today, dealing with the imperfect all about you. And, if everything you have now, imperfect as it seems and is, were suddenly taken away from you, the happiest day in your life would be when it was restored again to you.

"For the first time I've come to realize," said Jeb, "the beauty of the imperfect."

9

"CRAWLIDGE"

IT WAS "COUNTRY STORE" TIME. EVERYBODY WAS BUSY, and cars were parked all around the church. The ladies were preparing their annual turkey dinner, an event known round our little world. The churchyard was filled with pyramids of pumpkins, cabbages, and squash, bushels of fancy apples, tomatoes, and onions, baskets of peppers, potatoes, and corn. It was harvesttime, and offerings were brought in from the farms as donations to be sold and the money given to the church budget. There was a stand selling fresh cider, grape juice, and lemonade. There was a counter of baked goods—cookies, cakes, homemade bread, and all kinds of pies. People from the city were milling about buying winter supplies of fruits and vegetables.

"How much you figger, L. T.?" asked Zach Lamberton. "Good as last year?" L. T. was the country-store manager. He had once owned a store in Buffalo. He was busy setting prices, handling the money, and giving information.

"Well, kinda think so!" he ventured. "Last year we did better'n nine-fifty. We have close to seven-fifty now, and I'm countin' on a hundred more on apples and potatoes; the women usually bring in better'n a hundred and a quarter, and the stands ought to do another seventy-five. That'll come to about a thousand dollars."

"That's ten-fifty according to my 'rithmetic," checked Zach.

"Well—," L. T. was cautious, "you always have to figger on crawlidge."

If I remember correctly, I had heard L. T. use this same word once before. It had sifted through my mind, and I had forgotten. It was upon the occasion of making up our church budget, and estimating the pledges. The finance committee felt rather sanguine about our every-member canvass. There seemed to be enough promised to meet the expenses we anticipated; but L. T., who had acted as chairman, was not convinced. He talked about some of the members who meant well when they made their pledges, but were negligent and forgetful in paying them. Some promise but are trapped by unforeseen events and cannot make their promises good. Then he referred to unexpected expenses that come in during the year, higher prices. Then he added, "Whether it's money comin' in or goin' out, you've always got to figger on crawlidge."

This matter of "crawlidge" seems to fall into two main divisions—what we expect to receive from the world, and what we plan to give to the world.

"You've always got to figger on crawlidge," in what you expect to have from the world. Life also has its withholding tax, and many of life's bills receivable come discounted. A great number of its promissory notes are not as good as cash. People are most often too optimistic about their assets and not pessimstic enough about their liabilities. One early lesson the wise man learns is that he does not generally live as he wants to, but as he has to. Always there are modifying circumstances, and of all abilities, adaptability seems to be constantly called upon. Wherever one is, he must in certain things live as the Romans, friends, and countrymen do.

Brother Clarence Wells has finally decided to stay at Paw Paw. All along he has felt that he ought to take another charge. When we talked about his church and people, he was unhappy about two or three of his officers who were very critical of his work. Wherever he went in his parish, these were like gravel in his shoes. The other day when he came to see me, there was a new look of determination about him. I knew he had had his face lifted by some helpful experience. I was eager to learn about it, and soon he related how he had gone over to call upon one of the very men who had been critical of his work. He told him he had decided to ask for another church; that this officer and others seemed to be continually opposing his plans, holding back on things, pushing back in the breeching. Then the deacon, who was older, admitted some of the leaders, including himself, had been doing just that. He told Clarence that he was young, and like a young horse was full of energy, wanting to go places in a hurry.

"That holdin' back in the britchin' way you spoke," he said, "puts the matter right good. When the wagon is moving too fast, rolling downhill maybe, you've got to have holdback straps to keep the wagon from running away, from running right over the horses. Holdback straps are as important as tugs, if you're going to get anywhere."

Clarence had the mind to see the wisdom of this; but the

one thing that made him decide to stay was a statement the deacon made.

"Now, we'd like you to stay, Brother Wells. You can move, but you can't move out on people. Wherever you go, they'll be there; and sometimes it is better to change oneself a mite than to move off a hundred miles and change churches."

Clarence decided that changing himself was the easier move and made up his mind to stay. Life was a matter of give and take.

"You've always got to figger on crawlidge," when it comes to getting your rights. Cast your bread on whatever waters you may, and while some of it will come back—maybe a piece or two with jam on it—a certain percentage will be taken by the hungry fish. It may be well and right for you to have your just deserts, your proper recognition and due deference, but plan on being miserable if you are counting on measure for measure, a chicken for every egg. Some of your eggs may not hatch. No one sets the same price on you as you place on yourself. There is always a margin between what you hold yourself at and what others hold you to be. Count off a certain amount and charge it to "crawlidge." Rather, be prepared to make up the difference in humility. If you keep a margin of reserve, you will not often be embarrassed.

Herein lies the secret: Behold the aristocratic soul who not only expects a deficit might show up, and sets himself not to be too disappointed when it does come, but is prepared for it when it does with an ample reserve. Like the celebrated archer whose bowstring snapped. He might have shrugged his shoulders and sighed. "Well, that's to be expected; I can take it. Everyone has a little bad luck now and then." Maybe that is what he did say; and that would be commendable. But he did more. He deliberately took out a reserve cord for his bow, one he had been saving for such an emergency. He had planned on "crawlidge."

Life is a constant experience in dealing with shrinkage, leakage, and wastage. Obligations, demands, and expenses have a way of expanding and taking on unexpected proportions. The happy people are those who not only expect them but who also keep a bonus in store for meeting them. Even for the situations about which nothing can be done—say if the bowman had broken his arm—one can still keep in store the courage to face them.

One feels rich and increased in goods when the "crawlidge" he has figured on is not needed, when the balance is all in and he finds that the "crawlidge" is his to keep.

Take Dwight. Last summer he was planning his trip to the Holy Land. Being a minister, he had to count his coins carefully. "I have estimated all the cost of the trip, hotel expenses, food, and everything," he explained, "and I've added an extra one hundred dollars."

"What is that for?" I queried.

"That is to be cheated of. That way I go without worrying too much about not having enough to meet all the cost of the trip. I always feel safer that way."

When he returned in the fall and I was all ears to hear about the events of his trip, the glories of Jerusalem, the sanctity of Bethlehem and the hallowed land of Judea, the first thing he said was, "Remember the hundred dollars I took as reserve? Didn't have to use it at all. Isn't that something?" The hundred dollars "crawlidge" had made Dwight a rich man.

Life is not generally so considerate of our failure to figure on the unforeseen as the retired farmer who ran a motor court down on the Florida border. Jeb was telling about it. The owner was not in sight when he drove in, but then he showed up and Jeb asked him the price of his cabins.

"Which way you headed?" he asked.

"What's the difference?"

"There's a comin' price and a goin' price. Cabins is four dollars for them that's jest comin' into Florida on their vacations, and two dollars for them that's goin' home."

"Why's that?" asked Jeb.

"Well, I figger them that's comin' has plenty of money, but them that's goin' is likely almost broke. So I charge two prices, comin' and goin'."

"You've always got to figger on crawlidge." In the matter of what to expect from the world, "crawlidge" should be taken into consideration in living the good life. The writer of the wisdom literature in the Bible warns that "whoso breaketh an hedge, a serpent shall bite him" (Ecclesiastes 10:8). There is the germ of a whole sermon in this. Stay back from the hedge, he warns. There lie the serpents of evil. Plan on a margin between yourself and the thickets of sin. Make room for "crawlidge." So many good people walk so near the deep tangled wilds they become easy prey to the evil pythons.

Let your goodness have a margin. So many traverse the twilight zone that it is difficult to determine where they belong, difficult to discern between them and those who live in the bush. If one comes too near the hedgerow of evil, he endangers his virtue. Some evil snake may snag him. One should expect that and keep a "crawlidge" between himself and the dangers that lurk there. Maintain a safety zone of high moral conduct.

In second consideration, "you've always got to figger on crawlidge" in what you plan to give to the world. You will recall Madsen's rule to Dr. Johnson about having enough fruit in the orchard: "Enough to eat; enough to store up; enough to be stolen and enough to rot on the ground." And to that I should like to add, "Enough to share with others."

From old times it was a sacred injunction that the husbandman must cultivate enough to provide for others less fortunate than himself. The whole law of gleaning has this in mind. The corners must not be reaped; sheaves dropped must be left.

"You've always got to figger on crawlidge." Figure enough to spare of tolerance. The world is very short on this, and aristocrats of good living must make up the deficit. Bring this to bear in personal relationships. Be prepared to carry an extra supply of mercy. Be generous enough to include all, even the undeserving. Anyone can be kindly to the kind, can love the lovable. "If ye love them which love you, what reward have ye?" Yet more demanding is the admonition: "Love your enemies, bless them that curse you, do good to them that hate you." Good living is recognized by a mile. It keeps a mile of margin. It purposes that there shall be no mistake about it. It goes the second mile for "crawlidge."

In his counseling with couples who come to him to be

married, Brother Hathaway says he always warns them that in their home relationships they must not just count on meeting each other halfway. They must be prepared to go seventy-five per cent of the way. As L. T. would say, "You've always got to figger on crawlidge." Love expects more; and true love always gives more. Love "suffereth long, . . . seeketh not her own, is not easily provoked . . . ; beareth all things, . . . endureth all things." Not seventy-five per cent; "all things." It gives beyond expectation. Love never counts the cost.

In all giving, in all benevolence, count on shrinkage. People will discount your goodness. The world has become cynical. People may attribute your generosity to ostentation; to ulterior motive; to bidding for recognition; to escaping income tax.

The injunction is, "Freely ye have received, freely give." How exceeding "freely" we have received! God has counted on "crawlidge": "good measure, pressed down, and shaken together, and running over," "abundantly above all that we ask or think." He opens the windows of heaven and pours out his blessings. He gives to the unworthy as well as to the worthy; his graces fall on the just and the unjust. While men were yet sinners, he gave his chiefest gift. There was no survey as to worthiness. Here is love beyond all understanding. There was not just sufficient. Enough was not enough. There was more than adequate love, more than ample forgiveness.

In high moral living, then, both in receiving and in giving, in what you expect to receive from the world and in what you expect to give to the world, "you've always got to figger on crawlidge."

10

NEW OCCASIONS TEACH OLD DUTIES

HOWARD AND EDYTHE ALWAYS WANT PEOPLE TO KNOW that they are front row when it comes to the arts. They are patrons of the symphony, hold season tickets to the Orchestra Hall lecture course, attend all the current plays at the Lyceum, and seem to know all the latest books. I can't say they are overly popular because of their cultural pursuits. Indeed, I suspect many people try to avoid them. They often seem left alone. Perhaps it is because they use their knowledge in eccentric charges against Philistines in such a manner as to embarrass even their best friends.

Last evening, for example, Edythe, using her precise New England inflection—Edythe is not from New England, as everyone knows—called across the room, during a lull in the conversation, to Mabel, asking her if she had heard Professor Bellami's talk last night at St. Stephens Church on "The Revival of Majolica." Mabel, somewhat an artist in stripping the finery of pretense off those on parade, archly asked, "How many were converted, dear?"

Recently Howard did do me a service, as it turned out. He called right after dinner one evening to say that he had a couple of tickets to the exhibit at the Civic Art Gallery.

We went. Suds and I went and with lagging steps and eyes too full of seeing walked about the halls of many strange paintings. One or two, here and there, rewarded us with new strength and inspiration to go on. Mostly, however —and here my plebeian sackcloth is showing—I was unimpressed.

Then we came upon one that was the likeness of nothing in heaven above or in the earth beneath. We stood trying to credit the picture with some kind of meaning. I had already relegated the work to the limbo of the lost and nebulous, when at my elbow a voice, effulgent with admiration bordering on reverence, entoned, "Wonderful!"

Now, in a setting like this, one begins to suspect himself; perhaps he is color-blind, lame minded, and uncultured. I had felt that way before in many such situations and had walked away quite unhappy with myself. I was again about to do this when suddenly I felt something of resentment and a resolution becoming rigid within me. If I was a Mr. van Winkle, twenty years gone in slumber, it was high time for me to wake out of sleep and discover my blunderbuss opinions. This time I would not go away wondering about color blindness, my ability to appreciate beauty, or whatever it was.

At the first I was going to be ugly and resentful and say some such sarcastic thing as, "It looks like a mess to me." But if I was to learn, I must be respectful; and so I humbled myself and politely importuned the man, a very personable gentleman, to explain to me wherein lay the wonderfulness of this painting. I am not going to say that he succeeded in conveying to me the greatness of this particular picture, but he did give me one reasonable suggestion for modern art that I had previously written off as aberrations of the modern mind in painting, music, and literature.

His presentation was in the way of a lecture, and, to keep no one groping about, he was a lecturer—Professor Jules L'Estrange of the unversity art department.

The professor had some interesting metaphors: man is a chambered nautilus, restless to leave the low-vaulted past; man is an Abram, not content in his Ur, going out, not knowing where, but anywhere. Now, we see evidence all about us in the economic realm of this discontent. We see it in the world of philosophy and in literature and even in religion. What was said by them of old times was no complete word for those who would keep abreast of truth.

Man's desire to be free of the past, Professor L'Estrange ventured, is now breaking out in the arts. Of course, the lines and color are strange, but they are evidences of the rebellion against sameness. They deliberately set out to mock the lines of precision, balance, subordination, and perspective. In music there is a deliberate break with exact harmony, correct measure, and prettiness. Better is noise than monotony. In poetry this desire often results in an amorphous chaos of words signifying nothing but waiting to be molded into a new world of poetic expression. It is the cry of impatience against the old and the cry of longing for the new. It is rebellion, revolution, and the disturbance of a new world coming to birth. Certainly it is shocking, jarring, stabbing, and alarming; and it is disturbing our old complacency. Couldn't I see they are doing just that, that it is exceedingly effectual? This I had to admit. Also I had to confess that without this explanation much of modern art, music, and literature seemed to make no sense at all.

That was about the content of the professor's lecture as I recall it. Then, as if to bring his explanation to a fitting close, he shrugged his shoulders in a gesture of finality— " 'New occasions teach new duties,' *n'est-ce pas?*"

I began to think about that. Most of our neat aphorisms and quotations need further appraisal. So it was that the rest of my art-gallery visit became lost to me in my re-thinking this line of Lowell's. I finally came out with this amendment: New occasions also teach old duties!

The colter must go before the plow, and the harrowing must come before the planting; but there must also be the seed to plant, the good grains saved over from the old crop. And back of the old grains to be planted is yet the sun and the Father's will.

There must be the pioneers; but to colonize and hold the new discoveries, there must come the colony from the old-time settlement. On the other hand, the old would die without the new. The tree lives because the new leaves supplant the old. And back of the leaves that are yet to appear and those that fall today is the eternal, the continuing, that has no limiting past, present, or future.

Let some praise the modern, the new occasions, the new duties. Let others glorify the old, the past. I find myself thinking about both and coming to plead for what might be called the continuing mind, the attitude that hopes to conserve the past values to be used as the basis and incentive to lay hold on the future goods. The new occasions must not forsake the old duties. However modern the ship, it still will take the water to float it. However improved the airplane may be, it must make use of elements to lift it.

We must be careful not to make change an end in itself. Nothing is necessarily true, or false, because it is old; nothing invaluable or valueless because it is new. It would be an act of insanity to blow out the lights we have already lighted just to leap about, devil-may-care, in the dark. We cannot tell where we are going, or if we are going, if we fail to recognize where we have been.

Experience, "the one lamp" by which our feet are guided, has shown us that there are some things of old times that are to be treasured. We will have to hold on to them. New occasions will only teach their importance all over again.

When Grandmother Clarke died, it seemed the whole township came to her funeral. She was dearly loved. After she had gone, Nellie, her eighteen-year-old granddaughter, kept finding little notes she had left for her. One was found in the old cookbook: "I know how mad you get at that oven; it heats so slowly. I usually keep a supply of pine knots from the old stump fence handy." Once when Nellie burned her hand with hot grease, she found a note in the medicine chest: "For painful burns, I have found that tea will relieve the pain." For many years these little notes, echoes of the voice that was still, things tested by experience, kept popping up. When her wedding day came, Nellie went to find something "old" to wear, and to an old veil she found was pinned a little note, "Be happy, my dear. I'm sure I would love him too." So from the past came the love that does not die with death. So live on forever the eternal things that no new occasion could ever do without.

We must not mistake motion for progress, nor think that the god-of-things-as-they-are is always a devil. I do not by this make any plea to canonize a Saint Rip van Winkle. History affords many illustrations where standpattism has been the Cain of progress, stoning the prophets of old, martyring apostles of the new, and crucifying the messiahs. Change is neither to be hated as a sin nor worshiped as a god. I must learn to

> welcome each rebuff
> That turns earth's smoothness rough,
> Each sting that bids nor sit nor stand,
> but go!

But as I go, I must take some of the corn of the old harvest to be sure of the new. The new occasions will substantiate yet more firmly the good, beautiful, and true.

We must not imagine that we have mastered the old so well that we can afford to dispense with it. Because the child has now learned to walk, he does not forthwith give up walking; even in the automobile age, walking is still essential. Because the child has graduated from milk, he does not give up taking nourishment, even milk.

Withal, we have not put into practice all of the many things we know to be essential. Many lessons are known but not yet lived. Many of the sermons we have heard are not yet done; they have only been preached. The doing is yet to come.

Jeb says when the book agent went to call on Clem Ashley, he explained to Clem that the book he was selling would make him a better farmer than he had ever been. Clem refused to buy. He told the book salesman, "Can't use yer book. I'm not half as good a farmer now as I already know how to be." Many of the old duties are not yet mastered, and the new occasions will only cry out the need for their being carried out. The world knows better than it is acting. We are not half as good now as we know how to be. The new occasions will have to teach these old duties over and over again.

Now, the lessons of the old are not always lessons in goodness alone; they also in new occasions, and in new situations, will be there to remind us that many things that were evil under the old occasions are evil under the new; that not only is righteousness exalting, but also sin remains debasing. Though we may change our attitudes about things, the results are just the same. Phaëthon, driver of the sun chariot a long time ago, almost ruined the world one day, scorched off all vegetation in many places, making a desert, and drove so far off the road in other places that they have been frozen up ever since. That was the effect of alcohol back there, even when a god was driving and drank it, and it still has the same effect. Indulgence has sacked many a nation in the past, and although we have many new and modern vehicles and occasions, let us not be deceived. New occasions also teach old duties.

Of course the professor and the poet are right—new occasions do teach new duties. It is also true that new occasions will keep teaching the old duties. Not because they are old, but because they are eternal. Perhaps this is a better way of saying it: "New occasions also teach eternal duties." There are some old duties new occasions will never be able to change; nor should we want them to be changed. They cannot be changed because they are changeless, continuing. Let us keep not only the new mind but also the old mind, and strive, under God, to possess the continuing mind.

11

WON'T POWER

EMERSON, RECOGNIZED FOR HIS INTELLIGENCE, RELATES in his journal how he was balked by a stubborn calf. Anyone who has had any experience with these little barnyard bovines is at once sympathetic. He knows by experience the earth-rooted inertia of a stiff-necked, mulley calf. Mr. Emerson and his son were pulling and pushing, hauling and heaving, trying to get the little animal into the barn, but it was firmly planted, and its eyes were popping with cold determination. An Irish servant girl watched with amusement. After the savant and his son had surrendered to the beastie, she came forward and thrust her finger into the mouth of the calf. Nursing the servant girl's finger, the little animal followed her instantly into the stall. Wrote Mr. Emerson, "I like people who can do things."

The balky calf reminded me of Jess Clem's nag. "Nag" was the right word for this animal as applied to his conduct, but if you were describing his looks, he was a horse of a different color. He was attractive and of hippodrome appeal to look at; but he was a nasty, stubborn nag when it came to performance. He was balky. One day Jess sat in the middle of East Main Street in his buggy and read the *Globe-Democrat* from headlines to want ads while the plug stubbornly refused to move. A crowd gathered and "guyed" Jess. A few offered advice, but the horse stood like a statue. Jess had decided to sit it out if it took all summer and winter too, but a want ad changed his mind. A man selling sewing machines about the country wanted a horse, "strong and good looking." Jess decided here was an opportunity to get rid of this pigheaded horse. He noted the address and again began to try to get the horse to move. He used persuasive tones, sweet-smelling hay, corn on the cob, a feed bag of oats and sugar, all to no avail. Jeb told me the story: "Someone called out, 'Yer horse has got a lotta will power, Jess.' But as I saw it, it wasn't will power the critter had. It was won't power."

I had heard Jeb use this term before. It was at a church board meeting. Harry Clinton, our mayor, was present. He was the chairman of the board. After the business was finished, we sat around and visited. Suds was getting cider and doughnuts. Harry, who had been rather quiet, began talking about the affairs of his office. He said before he had become mayor, his temptations had been mostly of the fifty-cent to two-dollar variety, and easy to cope with; no trouble to turn down. Just that day he had had a $12,500 kind. The town was just putting in cement streets. A contractor offered Harry $7,500, then $10,000, and at last 2½ per cent if he would throw the contract his way. This last would have been $12,500, four times Harry's annual salary.

"Came pretty close to my price; got to thinking of a new house, car, and everything. I became scared, and had to tell that tempter to get out of my office."

"You've got a lot of will power, Harry," I suggested.

"Not will power," commented Jeb, "won't power."

"I like people who can do things," said Mr. Emerson. Of course, we all do. We celebrate the doers, the men of action. Moses led the children of Israel out of Egypt. Joshua "fit de battle of Jericho." Elijah slew the prophets of Jezebel. Nehemiah rebuilt the walls of Jerusalem. Columbus discovered America. Washington crossed the Delaware. But these men could also be honored for what they would not do. Moses refused to be called the son of Pharaoh's daughter. Joshua would not bring back a cowardly report. Elijah disdained bowing the knee to Baal. Nehemiah scorned compromise with Sanballat, because he was doing a great work for the Lord and could not come down. Columbus flatly declined the appeals and threats of his crew that he turn back. Washington rebuffed the demand of the British that he surrender. These were great men also because of the things they refused to do.

"I like people who can do things," wrote Mr. Emerson, and I am certain that he would and did like also the men who would not do things—men who have won't power, according to Jeb. The world has been saved by will power, no doubt, and many times also by men of sterling won't power.

Let us recognize that a great deal of won't power is wasted on unimportant things, in relationship to things that are of small or negligible consequences. Life has been cluttered with many taboos. Sacrifices are made to keep them, some even unto death, and more is the pity. We are led to admire the courage behind such sacrifices even though we question the value.

Lem Castle was young and a very good man in his way,

a solid citizen and a deacon in a small church down Pond Creek way. He and Ethel Bailey had been going together for about three years. It seemed a likely match. They never did get married. Broke off altogether. It seemed she refused to marry him because he wouldn't wear a necktie. He wore a collar but no tie. It had something to do with his religious persuasion. Ethel wouldn't because he wouldn't. Two won't powers. Perhaps both of small value. When love is unable to bring about a compromise, one realizes the force of won't power. If it could only be harnessed to pull on tugs instead of the holdback straps!

Now this can bring about dire results. May 10, 1857, brought about the Sepoy Mutiny in India. The East India Company was unable to control things, and the British government had to take over. The native soldiers were supplied with ammunition. The soldiers, *Sipahi*, had to bite off the end of the cartridges. These were covered with grease. The religion of the Hindus forbade taking into the mouth anything from the cow, and the religion of the Mohammedans anything from the swine. The British command thought it was unimportant, and a revolt occurred. There followed the cruel massacre at Cawnpore.

Virtue falls victim when the consequence of refusing to break with taboo is greater evil than the value of keeping it. What profit is it if a man be so intent on worshiping his gods that he destroy his fellow men? How can that which serves not man be a service to God? What value is bread, however holy, if a David is hungry? What value a day, however sacred, if it forbids the healing of the sick? A great deal of won't power is squandered on things that matter very little and are often of no consequence at all.

But there are some things that must not be done; for which won't power is a saving thing.

> Let it be said when life is through,
> Some things there were I would not do.[1]

Of late years we have become a little soft and lax. There has been a strong emphasis on expression in education, an antipathy against repression. Let the children grow up un-inhibited. Never tell them that they can't do anything.

Cora Gay was an authority on expression in education. She never believed in interfering with the will of children; to do so, she thought, would blight their personality. They must be allowed to grow up unrestrained. Cora was quite a speaker on this, having taken a course on child psychology at the state university. The guild had engaged her to speak at its Tuesday meeting. When the hour came for her speech, she was not present. The president of the guild attended to all the business, had a half-hour of community singing, and anxiously watched the door. Cora finally came, after almost an hour's delay. With her she brought her small daughter. She apologized for her tardiness and explained, "I started in ample time. It is, after all, only a few blocks; but Coralee, my little daughter here, insisted on going up to every house and ringing the doorbell, and I just could not tell her not to do it for fear of limiting and stunting her individuality."

Now, I am sure our expressionists find objection to this. Cora should have given her daughter something else to engage her attention. She might have gone straightway to

[1] From a poem copyrighted by Edgar A. Guest. Used by permission of the Reilly & Lee Co.

the store and bought her daughter a bell to ring. But Cora-lee might have refused to go along, and she couldn't just leave her. Somebody had to remain and apologize to the householders who answered the door. She might have given her her coin purse to jingle, but women's purses have such a habit of popping open all the time. Or, maybe the ring of her voice might have stopped the child. In any case it would have been different from the way Aunt Amanda Brown said she did: "I raised my children with a barrel stave and I raised 'em frequent."

Certainly expression is a strong factor in life. But there are some things we cannot let children practice expression upon. Their personalities will have to be limited by accepting some authority, or their lives will be permanently limited. Some things they had better not be allowed to try out for themselves, even once. Like taking a drink from the ammonia bottle in the laundry, or poking their tiny fingers in to investigate an electric socket, or jumping out of the second-story window. At some point they must come up against a positive negative: There are some things that must not be done.

Adults face this every day. There are traffic lights that must not be raced through. There are laws that must not be transgressed. There are liberties that must not be taken. Men have paid dearly to learn by trial and error. "Thou shalt not steal"; "Thou shalt not kill"; not because God or man wants to be arbitrary and throw around weights of authority, but because it is expedient, it is best for everyone.

There are areas where man cannot be just neutral. It would mean death. For public safety there are steps of discipline that must be taken. There are viruses, bacteria, and germs that we cannot be passive about. We must take the position that we won't have them.

The little religious community at Claybrook had some religious scruple against vaccinating for diphtheria. But the county medical authorities could not be neutral about this without endangering the health of adjacent communities. Diphtheria is no respecter of persons.

So it is in the moral world. Some things are wrong, deadly. There has been a great deal of playing fast and loose with ethical values. Some cults have assured that there is no such thing as evil; that all is good.

Brother Stemper of Beulah church in the city was sitting at breakfast one Sunday morning when the doorbell rang. When he went to the door, there stood a small boy. He was poorly clad. He told Brother Stemper that he had come to ask him to go to the jail and talk with his father. His father was to go to the electric chair on Monday for the murder of the boy's mother. Brother Stemper went, and the poor man stumbingly told his story. He had no recollection of his deed. He had been under the influence of liquor. Brother Stemper tried to console the man with scripture and prayer. Following the execution he made the funeral arrangements and took the three orphaned children to their father's funeral. Then the children were sent to an orphans' home. Brother Stemper had been a soldier in World War I. In telling the story he said, "I fought to save my country from the enemy outside, but we have an insidious enemy here at home that I must engage."

The world is often saved by the men of unconsenting conscience. Virtue is saved for the world by men who refuse to stand for vice, men who will not allow their hatred of evil to fall into disrepair. Everything cannot be loved. If we love some things, we must of necessity hate others. "Ye that love the Lord, hate evil." Indescribable tragedy can befall a man when he has come to love the things he ought to hate, loving the evil and hating the good. In the final sum of things perhaps all sin is, is just the absence of enough hate.

The man of sterling worth must make up his mind to refusal. Learn to say, "I won't." He will have to be willing to see other people do things without any seeming scruple, and still hold his position. Other apparently good people may practice dishonesty and seem to get away with it; but he cannot. Others of good standing may cheat and lie, say malicious things about innocent people; but he cannot. Others who are creditably accepted may have no scruples against speaking out against other races and religions. He cannot do it. Others may laugh at convention and think nothing of playing free and easy with moral standards and marital fidelities. He cannot. And if he dares, he will lose the profound respect he holds of himself and betray God's confidence in his integrity.

Settle it then; this is a time for great won't power; for strong refusal.

"I like people who can do things," said Mr. Emerson. Certainly he knew the moral strength and worth of the men who refused to do the compromising. "Won't power," says Jeb.

12

PRACTICING WITHOUT
PREACHING

I WENT TO MR. CHAMPLIN'S FUNERAL. ALMOST EVERYONE
in the community attended. Gabe Champlin was an un-
commonly good man. He was not an exhibitionist, but
quietly and powerfully a good man. Good, not in the sense
of being harmless, but good and useful, good and helpful.
In going to the funeral I had a chance to be a layman for a
change. Brother Hathaway preached the sermon. He did
not so much preach a funeral sermon as praise the departed
man. In eulogizing Gabe's good living he used the text,
"Well done, thou good and faithful servant." And there was
a kind of symphonic recurrence that he kept using: "I tell
you Brother Champlin was one man that practiced what
he preached."

"You know," Jeb said, as we walked home together,
"I didn't so much care for Brother Hathaway's saying that
Gabe was one man that practiced what he preached. He
didn't. He never preached. Gabe was no talker. I wonder
if the preacher wouldn't have been nearer the truth about
Gabe if he'd just said, 'He never preached what he practiced.'"

"That's a new thought," I rejoined. "But, even putting it that way, it still detracts nothing from the goodness of the man."

"Indeed it does not," he amplified. "It adds to his virtue. It takes courage to keep your goodness going without calling attention to it. Besides, there is so much of preaching in the world anyway, we need more people who hold opinions."

"That includes almost everyone," I said. "All of us hold opinions."

"There you're wrong," said Jeb. "Very few hold opinions. Opinions are hard to hold—easy to let go of. You're not with anybody very long until he lets fly with an opinion."

That was his way of further attesting to the strength of character of Gabe Champlin. I gave this some thought. Strength of character does lie in reserve power—keeping one's resources in store and never completely expending the whole of them. A forceful personality does not need to make ostentatious display. It would indicate something of a weakness to drag out a cannon to dispense with a mosquito. Many are the talented ones who have abundant ability, but convince few people and seem to have few friends because they erupt so effusively that everyone runs for cover. When their point might be made with a word, they make a lecture out of it. Often the situation might better be gained by saying nothing and doing a timely deed.

To be sure, there are those who don't preach what they practice simply because they are timorous and haven't the courage of their convictions. They let their "dare not" scare off their "would." Then there are those who never preach because they have no convictions at all. Generally convictions make one very courageous. Shepherds, carpenters, and fishermen have faced up to tyrants, "quenched the violence of fire," "stopped the mouths of lions," and "turned to flight the armies." It seems to be the unsure who are hesitant; they are the cowardly, because they are unconvinced. If one is certain, he is eager to champion. If he believes, he is bound to propagate his belief. Often he "cannot but speak" the things he has seen and heard; he is unable to refrain from preaching. One might as well say, "Quiet," to a storm and expect the sun to break through. It must thunder. If he preaches not, it might indicate that he believes not. Or, it might be that he has learned a more excellent way of declaring his faith—the way of deeds—and finds it much more convincing.

"He never preached what he practiced." As Jeb said, there is so much of preaching today. The world is full of many voices, and Babel has become a mountain that has filled the whole earth. Of the making of sermons there is no end. One of the illustrations Brother Hathaway used in the funeral talk was a personal reference, an experience he had with his little five-year-old granddaughter. She was always eager for a story, and one evening after he had told her one at bedtime, she asked him, "Grandpa, was that a true story, or were you just preaching?" So it is that people become suspicious of our much speaking. Maybe what we talk so much about is only a fairy story.

Virtue often loses its appeal when attention is called to it. "It takes courage to keep your goodness going without calling attention to it," said Jeb. It becomes a display of selfishness. Into the same category might go such things as displaying a religious symbol, wearing a holy garb, using unctuous phrases in ordinary conversation—especially with those who know you best, cultivating a pious tone, talking down to people in a manner that assumes that you are saved and they are lost.

The bishop preached for Brother Hathaway one Sunday and quite inadvertently stated something facetious, but worth thinking about. Likely in his moment of reaching for something further to say, he remarked, "The doctrine of salvation, as I understand it, is not very well understood." And which one of us understands it so well that he may use the sanctimonious tone in judging anyone's doctrine or life? Which one is without sin?

Into this same category, also, may be placed the unsightly daubing of rocks along the roadway with holy sayings, passing out religious literature printed on cheap paper. There are mediums of preaching that are often unworthy of the dignity of the gospel we profess. Apparently it is not enough to be only good; we must be good in the right way. Overreligious people can be as repulsive as overdressed people, gaudy and cheap.

One night after a midweek service at which I had given a talk on Ecclesiastes 7:16 ("Be not righteous over much"), Mike Odle said whimsically, "I'm right sorry for God. He not only has his problems with the evil people in the world, but some of the righteous are enough to make even God give up in despair. I wouldn't wonder, if we could hear the angels talking, they might be saying, 'We'd had the sinners all won long ago if it hadn't been for the saints; about time we get one decided, some overreligious church member starts preaching at him and scares him plumb away.' I never believed so thoroughly before in the insecurity of the saints."

That ministers are likely to be guilty of too much preaching, is to say the obvious. Mark Twain, or whoever it was who took the fifty cents out of the collection box, represents a great number of people who grow tired of too much sermonizing. One of the sad things is that an evangelist with "forty-parson power" might well win a hundred to the church and, in the same effort, alienate a thousand others who will have nothing further to do with religion if his preaching is a true sample of it.

"He never preached what he practiced." That was a very thoughtful way of putting it about Gabe Champlin. But Jeb was wrong about that. Who can practice goodness without preaching it? What is more eloquent than action? What is more convincing than a deed? Few are the recorded sermons of the Galilean, if indeed there is one complete one. He "went about doing good." His life was a ceaseless sermon. To his followers the command was, "As ye go, preach." Sermons in shoes. Sermons are much better that are done up in living skin than in any of the best bindings. Probably for this cause, Gabe never preached orally. He knew there was something greater than good preaching—for that matter, better than good writing, and in that sense, better than scripture itself—and that was convincingly good living. He would not make his gospel vain by preaching about it. Things may also be destroyed by speaking about them. How eloquent is a good clean bed! How articulate a pair of mended hose, how convincing a tasty dinner! But if one should hear, "That was a good job I did for you in giving you a nice clean bed," or, "That was a wonderful dinner I prepared for you," something would be lost. "It takes courage to keep your goodness going without calling attention to it." When we call attention to it, the natural- ness of the deed is lost, its perfume blown away, and it is not any more appealing than paper flowers.

Tradition has it that when the Queen of Sheba visited King Solomon, famed for his wisdom, she tested his ability upon many occasions. Once she had brought in before the king two great bouquets of roses. One was artificial; one was real. She challenged the wise man to choose which were the natural roses, judging from the throne where he sat. Solomon commanded that some bees be brought in. They settled immediately upon the true flowers. So does the wise old world detect quickly that which is artificial and false. Men have a sense for the true.

If someone is hoping that I shall quote the scripture, "Be ye doers of the word," I now oblige. But I should like to add a revision which I could hope James would add were he to write again, and it is, "Be ye be-ers of the word." A man must be to do. If he is, he does. And when he does because he is, he is most genuinely convincing to everyone. With men it is what the "is" does that counts. They discern that his actions are not acting. They are beautifully natural, like the bouquet of true roses.

"He never preached what he practiced." No, he didn't need to. Words would be superficial, overdecorative. A rose needs no red paint. "Rose is a rose is a rose is a rose." The true life is its own best sermon.

13

TALEHEARERS AND TALEBEARERS

Suds had gone to the front window several times. I could see her each time she passed the study door. I began to wonder what was disturbing her patience; then I remembered it was the day for the cleaning woman to come. This was verified when with evident relief she murmured, "Well, at last Mary Ellen is coming."

Mary Ellen was a village institution, tall, strong, and erect. She moseyed along with a queenly dignity, usually crowned by a huge bundle of laundry balanced on her head. Ray Dunn once remarked that he was happy at last his daughter Hildred had found some use for a book. She was using it to give herself poise, walking about the house with it balanced on her head. Mary Ellen had a stateliness that her burden gave her. Responsibilities, gracefully carried, always give one poise. We walk the world with dignity when we have a load to carry. Irresponsibility is always graceless and unbecoming. Kingly is the man who wears his obligations like a tiara; "so nigh is grandeur to our dust." It always gives man a lift when he lifts something. When he carries a duty well, it carries him.

The door opened—Mary Ellen didn't bother to knock— and her strong arms easily lifted the huge bundle of clean clothes from her head. She tied on the apron Suds handed her, found the cleaning utensils, and began her work.

Mary Ellen might have thought of herself as the oral reporter for the neighborhood. Wherever she went, from home to home, she carried the secrets of each family with her. Her tongue usually outworked all other muscles. It is possible that part of her acceptance as a cleaning woman in so many homes lay in the desire of some of her employers to hear the latest news.

I could hear her now: "That woman peels her potatoes thinner than any woman I ever worked for; then her man wonders why his hogs ain't gettin' fat."

While in some homes her recitals may have been received with interest and encouragement, I felt that Suds would usually let Mary Ellen ramble on without hearing what was being said. It was like preparing windfall apples for cooking—when you peeled them, cut away the rotten places, and took out the core, there wasn't too much left. Later that morning Suds must have offered some word of caution to Mary Ellen, for I heard her talking in an injured tone.

"But all my other ladies seem to want me to open up with all the news of the places where I been workin.' I'm not aimin' to be what you call a talebearer."

"I know, Mary Ellen, I know," replied Suds. "You don't mean any harm. I just don't want to hear about other people's affairs. You know, if there were no talehearers, there would be no talebearers."

Here is another application of the law of supply and demand. If there were no demands, suggested Suds, people who wanted to hear gossip, it would limit the production considerably. No babblees, no babblers.

As to the supply, there seems to be gossip unlimited. There are many talebearers; indeed, there seems to be something of the private investigator in all of us. Maybe we take comfort in discovering that there are others who are also vulnerable. We become adept in confessing other people's sins. Touch a man anywhere and get a story. Everyone seems to have a little supply of gossip; everyone seems to be a peddler. A little lump of gossip is like yeast; it quickly leavens the whole countryside. It grows. It can put two and two together and get a dozen. So the supply is abundant.

Talebearing can be very pernicious, as criminal as stealing. As the poet suggests, stealing a purse is but taking trash compared with filching away another's good name. It can be as foul as murder. Once another has been killed, that is the end of him; but scandal is living murder; killing people while they remain alive. By this measure one can be guilty of a hundred murders. Many good and great are delivered unto death every day. The character assassin is the most vicious of criminals.

The talebearer had better be sure of the product he is marketing. Unfortunately, rumor can be more convincing than reality, and just as deadly. It is best to be certain of the facts; even then, if it is not necessary, not conditionally revealed, not truth spoken in love, it can be harmful.

Almost everyone knew Harry Clinton. He was a home boy and worked every day at the box factory. He didn't seem too well, but he kept on the job. He wasn't much of one to attend church. Then rumor, always two days ahead of the printed news, was spread that Harry had been seen dead drunk, lying in the bushes near the park. That story was killed. When the local paper came out on Thursday, the headline read, "Harry Clinton's Life Saved." Harry was a diabetic. That day he was seen "drunk" by the many people who passed by and clucked their tongues, he had fallen into a coma. He might have died, but a certain nurse passed that way, stopped to examine him, recognized his danger, quickly secured some candy, and revived him.

What we see is often what we are looking for. The ancient nursery rhyme conveys this idea. The cat took a trip to London to see the queen and only saw a mouse under her chair. But what of the queen? The palace? Westminster? It is to be expected, tabby cats look for mice.

What we hear is often what we are listening for. John Summers went to New York City to visit some of his relatives. They were walking along in Times Square when suddenly he told them that he heard a cricket. "Nonsense, in this rumble and roar of traffic, it would be impossible to hear a cricket," was their comment.

John took a quarter out of his pocket and dropped it on the walk, and instantly every head within forty feet turned to see who had dropped some money. "See," he said, "people hear what their ears are trained to hear."

There is a blessed deafness, a happy blindness. Mr. Edison was thankful to be cloistered from all the small talk; he knew if anyone tried to make him hear, it must be important. If we could train ourselves to hear the worthful, the good, it could be said of us, "Blessed are your ears, for they hear" the things of life eternal. If we could train our eyes to see the beautiful and the true, it could be said of us, "Blessed are your eyes, for they see."

As we see, as we hear, so we tell. If we see and hear falsely, we speak falsely. There is even a more devious, nefarious kind of falseness. We may see and hear correctly, but have a crooked mind, with a crooked tongue to minister, and the truth comes out twisted. The lie is not in the seeing or hearing, but in the saying. We tell things not the way they are, but the way we want them to be. The astigmatism is in the mind; the shadow is in the heart.

Hearts can be so dark that they can pass over great deeds of kindness, to condemn a point of small consequence. Everyone should have been happy that the man was healed. He had been infirm for years; now he was made well. But the healing only brought condemnation, because it had occurred on the Sabbath. The mote of contention was of greater value than the beam of goodness. With eyes so crooked, ears so stopped, and mind so twisted, it is small wonder that for right seeing, right hearing, and right thinking there must be a new man.

"If there were no talehearers, there would be no talebearers." How shall the supply be cut off? Can we deal with the matter from the supply end? Kill the supply and the traffic will die? That is doubtful.

In working a crossword puzzle Jeb came across the word "brank." The dictionary defines it as a gossip bridle used by the Puritan fathers to try to control the tongue. It fastened over the head and under the jaws, holding the mouth shut, and it had a steel plate with barbs on it that was inserted in the mouth. It was very painful when one tried to move the tongue. Apparently it was not too successful. To stop talebearing completely, everyone might have to be "branked." Prohibition of speaking, besides being impossible to carry out, would prove to be a detriment to the world. Still, the warning is that if any man bridle not his tongue, his religion is vain. And Mary Ellen ought to know that this also applies to women.

"If there were no talehearers, there would be no tale-bearers." There seems to be an inexhaustible supply; what about the demand? Can this be stopped? Can we eliminate the talehearers?

Talehearers seem to be in abundance. Telephones are clogged at the receiving end. Newspapers that are full of tale-bearing find plenty of circulation. Confession magazines are trying to pump out enough tales to meet the market demand. It seems there is a hunger unsatisfied, a thirst unquenched. A recent cartoon showed two women boarding an airplane, and one of them was saying to the hostess, "You are not going to fly faster than sound, are you? We've got a lot of gossiping to do."

It is a vicious habit, talehearing, and many are the addicts. Plenty of people are looking for a "fix" with fixed ears. Many are the repeaters. It gets to be a disease that affects the ears, and the disease is epidemic. People pass gossip on to others usually in enlarged doses.

What, then, can be done about the menace of talehearing? Talebearing might be limited if there could be set in motion a general strike against hearing tales. President Grant sometimes did this. Once when a Cabinet member suggested that he had a tale to tell and observed that there were no ladies present and he would proceed with his story, the President refused to be a talehearer. There were no ladies present, he observed, but there were gentlemen. There might be a general embargo against talebearing set up by the talehearers. It would certainly have some results. It would have some effect on talebearing if people refused to be told.

There is another method. Talebearing could be encouraged. We might take the positive approach. Elder Mowbridge surprised his people by announcing that he loved to have people talk about him, provided what they said about him was good. Instead of trying to curb the wild horse of talebearing, one might ride him, harness him, put him to work to condition the soil for the sowing of good seed. Ride him out everywhere proclaiming the good news. Certainly there must be an adequate supply of nice things to say. Be a talebearer, but be certain the tale that is borne is a good one.

The bishop seems to be practicing something of this method. Recently when we were together, Tom Garroway suddenly began in a hushed tone, "I heard a good one the other day—"

"Wait a minute, Tom," interrupted the bishop. "Is this a good one?"

Come to think of it, we must have gone on to something else. I don't remember that Tom told his story after all.

There ought to be ample supplies of good things to say, and we should keep them in mind as assiduously as we seem to remember the bad things. We are none of us exempt from the evil things, but surely there are redeeming features about every one of us. We had a little redhead in our family. She is grown now. We called her our pink lady. Once she came in with a strangle hold on a very mottled alley cat, with a calico coat of many colors. It was a sad excuse for a feline. She dropped the cat, which recovered its dignity immediately and began calling for something to eat. When she was admonished to get that ugly cat out of the house, she replied, "But it does have a cute miaow. Couldn't we keep it?"

Let us keep in mind the happy things to say. Bear tales to people of other people's best qualities rather than their poorest. One would think that a woman who had five living husbands and was living with a man to whom she was not married would be a choice subject for the gossip mongers. But there was good in that woman of Sychar. It was quickly discovered and brought to light.

Let talebearing be unrestrained. Let the supply and demand grow. Go everywhere giving the good news. Refuse to sit in the scorner's seat, to walk "in the counsel of the ungodly."

There you are, Mary Ellen. Be a good talebearer, for "thou shalt not go up and down as a talebearer" of evil among the people (Leviticus 19:16). And I warrant, Suds, that if there are talehearers that insist on hearing the good about people, there will be talebearers carrying the good news.

14

"SWEAR NOT AT ALL"

"It's raining; so you take Maude and Dolly to Ab's for shoeing. Get started early. There'll be a line today."

For me, as a boy on the farm, a rainy day was brighter than the sunny ones. It might mean harness mending, wagon greasing—anything different from field work in the broiling sun. But best of all was a visit to the smithy's forge, the huffing and puffing bellows, and the meteor glow of the arcing sparks from blows struck while the iron was hot.

I had to wait in line despite the early start. Busy farmers were taking advantage of the rainy day. Ab Kazmayer, the blacksmith, was a village character. He was his usual surly self. Whenever more work came in for him to do, he seemed to resent it. His soot-smeared face, blackened by stubby beard, was made yet darker with the frown of annoyance. When I led in the gray mares, his temper came to its critical point and his booming voice shook the shop.

"I'll be sanctified!" he said, and perhaps I should note that I have edited his remarks a little. "You back here again with them blessed mares! Why in paradise can't you come when it's not raining? You've not a worshipful thing else to do. I got more'n I can graciously handle today."

He went right ahead and began preparing the hooves for fitting. I made no reply. Like all the neighbors, I knew how to "take old Ab." His growl, there was no bite in it. He was a craftsman and knew how to handle the iron. People recognize people who know how to do their work; craftsmanship wins for itself a great deal of tolerance. Ab was a craggy man, sinewy and rough. I can never remember him when he was dressed up. When on Sunday he threw himself into the corner of the rear pew, he still looked like Ab the smithy. People of the community knew it was "old Ab's way of sayin' things," and that he meant no harm.

It was Amos Kendall, himself a deacon in the church, who set me to thinking about Ab and the habit he had of swearing. He said, "Old Ab is the cussingest man I ever knew, but I never heard him swear in my life." It may have been a distinction without a difference. Ab seemed to do a pretty good job in both "cussin'" and swearing, as far as I could judge. But it set me to thinking about this ubiquitous habit of man.

If we think of swearing as using God's name in vain, a great many more people are swearing than think they are. One might use God's name as a benediction in such a vituperative manner that it would sound like a malediction instead. A panhandler solicited Jeb in the city one day, and when he was refused, he snarled, "Well, God bless your soul." It was said in such a manner that Jeb said he felt he had been sworn at.

One might use God's name in vain by blessing things that should be cursed. Many are the people who use God's name as endorsing their faiths—faiths that would scandalize the holy Deity, belie his character, and libel his name.

One might take the name of God in vain by claiming to be his follower and living in such a manner as to be a total discredit to the Eternal.

Swearing as calling God to witness is biblical. Many are the injunctions of the Scriptures about swearing. A handy concordance would be very convincing of this. There is one requisite: care must be taken to swear by the true God (Isaiah 65:16). There must be no recognition of false gods, for seeing we deify and make that our god by which we swear, therefore we forsake the true God if we swear by "them that are no gods" (Jeremiah 5:7). A case might be made for swearing properly; taking God's name usefully. It is the vain use of the holy name that is reprehensible.

Paul Van Dyke's *George Washington* reports that General Scott was asked, "Did Washington swear?"

"Yes, sir," he replied, "he did once at Monmouth, and on a day that would make any man swear. Yes, he swore that day until the leaves shook on the trees; charming, delightful. Never have I enjoyed such swearing before or since. Sir, that day he swore like an angel from heaven."

If one may speak about the impunity of righteous anger, there may also be some place for righteous swearing.

A great many of the most virtuous people apparently feel the need of using expletives and execrations that are often said with as heavy emphasis as evil swear words might be; indeed, most of them are counterfeit swear words, borderline copies of the real, ersatz swearing. "By gosh," "Gol darn," "Dad gum," "Gosh dang it," are thin imitations of the real thing. And even the more polite terms have implications: "Gee," for Jesus; "Zounds," "God's wounds"; "Blimey," for "God strike me blind"; "Bloody," for "By our Lady"; "Lawsamassey," for "Lord have mercy." Are the people who use these terms less culpable, more moral, than those who use the more definite terms? Couldn't they possibly be even more blameworthy than the cursers, if they use these parlor oaths with more of choler, with more of an evil spirit?

Why doesn't someone attempt a new vocabulary of imprecations? Those so often used are overworked. Apparently there is a need for proper words to adequately express temper and emotion; to leech the mind of tumorous blood. Maybe someone could coin some new phrases that might prove to be without any implications of using the Deity's name in vain. Tarkington in *The Fighting Littles* introduces a new phrase that might be used: "You jobjam, dobdab fool." This seems to be, however, somewhat borderline, and might prove a little indelicate for some who are more scrupulous. Ward Steinbeck always used a favorite expression describing someone he thought worthy of being trimmed down to size: "Why, he's a cockarumdum idiot." Now, one might spend a little time on this developing terms for blowing off splenetic heat. On a rainy afternoon when you had so carefully planned on having an outdoor picnic, instead of using the timeworn "Oh, for gosh sakes," which is also quite suggestive of irreverence, you might just "r'ar back" and shout, "Oh, galoshes and dumbrella!" Take an occasion when you are more inclined to threaten than to fight with fists—you could shout at the one with whom you are annoyed, "I'll knock the very belladabklap out of you"; or you might try, "You low-down hoblorhizapod"; and he might be more inclined to buy a dictionary than to strike you. There is plenty of room for phrase making: "You demoslopagog!"

But withal, even these words with no unholy connotation, no slander on the Deity, can often be said with even more spite and hatred, and more of sin, than forthright swearing. It is the spirit that molds the meaning. Like Ab, one may be the "cussingest" kind of man and never swear at all, and one might never swear and be the lowest kind of "cuss."

The wiser word has already been spoken: "Swear not at all." The counts against swearing are many.

It is a corruption of good manners. This may be the weakest count; but there are many who are less sensitive to the laws of Moses than they are to the amenities of the social set, many who have a drawing-room code that must not be broken. They would prefer to be accused of bad ethics rather than bad taste. In any case, most people want to appear well behaved, and perhaps this count is not so weak as it is first supposed, since it takes us away from the realm of moral consideration. Belching in public has no moral implications, but it is vulgar. Probably no one is damned for spitting on the sidewalk, but it is coarse and ugly. So it is that swearing is seldom considered a mark of good breeding. It cheapens good conduct and sets a poor example.

Secondly, swearing indicates a low balance in adequate vocabulary; one is bankrupt of rich words. The same tongue-worn stereotypes are ridiculously used over and over again. If it is cold, it is "damn" cold; if it is hot, it is "damn" hot. This indicates a distressing poverty. As Jeb says about his old dog Shep, "That dog can say more with his tail than most people can with their tongues and the whole English language for their use."

Again, swearing is taking unfair advantage of others; demanding that people make allowances. As it was always said, "Well, everybody knows how to take Old Ab." Too many people already draw upon the bank of public tolerance for needed coverage. Why make continuous and unnecessary demands on the world's forgiveness? Think of the numberless injustices people have to put up with. Why conduct yourself on the low level where everybody must make adjustment when you are around; as if you had some repulsive body odor or some foul contagion? And here we come upon the ethical relationships, moral conduct. The words of the Golden Rule might be interpreted to read, If you do not want others to swear in your presence, do not swear in theirs.

"Swear not at all. . . . But let your communication be, Yea, yea; Nay, nay; for whatsoever is more than these cometh of evil." The Author of these words himself felt the need for using strong maledictions: "serpents," "generation of vipers," "whited sepulchres." But his judgments were true, and his doctrine still holds.

Expletives often indicate deception; extra words are used to camouflage the false; such may be clever but still fall into the classification of lying. Truth is simple, "yea and nay." Deception is lavish with words.

"Swear not at all." This is quite final. One basic reason behind this curt command is that truth needs no support, not even divine certification. Truth is its own notary. If it is true, it cannot be made more true by adding expletives, or by calling upon God to damn those who refuse it. Truth's yea is yea; its nay, nay.

A second reason lies in the fact that when one is most deeply under the conviction of truth, most radically moved, he makes no long speeches. He does not seek to induce his emotions; he is already possessed by them. His "yea" is so irresistibly yea, it needs no assistance from adjectives; his "nay" so immovably nay, he feels no need to bring in oaths. And those who hear him need them not to know the man's unassailable position. He would but wound and destroy his cause by stooping to cloying verbiage. Everyone knows here is no situation for extra words. Just as they did when Patrick Henry and Abraham Lincoln spoke. Just as they did before the truth of the mighty Galilean. What they said was so completely true, and their hearts so utterly sincere, they could not but use simple language.

And finally, the reason for the terse injunction, "Swear not at all," lies in the fact that a fallible human being calling upon God to damn, arrogates a power he does not possess. If God damned at every human behest, what a pitiable hell we should have on earth! God is no errand boy, no trigger man for mortals to use at beck and call.

Well, of course, we know how to "take old Ab. It's just his way." We bear with all the Abs in the world. They likely "mean no harm." But the burden of the world would be much easier, and Ab himself even better liked as a man, if he followed a little closer the warning, "Swear not at all."

15

"TO BE LITTLE
IS TO BE LITTLE"

Elbert reed, the baptist minister over at mendon, tells a droll story about his little daughter Beth. It may be apocryphal, as many pulpit stories are, not true as to fact but true in application. They had taken Beth to a service of baptism at Dorris' Pond. She was quite impressed. The next day they found her having a baptismal service all her own. The candidates were her kittens. She had filled a hole in the ground with water. Holding the little animal over the hole, she was saying, "I baptize you in the name of the Father, Son, and in-the-hole-he-goes."

The learning ability of the young mind is amazing. Often, however, many of the expressions and sayings are not fully understood and sometimes may remain strangely twisted. "Say fancy cure," were the words of one of the church-school hymns I sang as a child. Much later, when I had learned to read them in the hymn, "Leaning on the Ever-lasting Arms," they changed for me and took on meaning —"safe and secure."

When I was a small boy, Nora was our cleaning woman. She came on Fridays. She had a saying she often used:

"To be little is to be little." That is the way I heard it, and the way she would say it, it sounded quite meaningful and always seemed to be full of wisdom. But to me it did not seem to say much. I would often repeat it to try to catch her meaning, even to the point of saying it just as she did, "Well, I always say, to be little is to be little." It made little sense to me. It didn't appear to be worth the breath to say it. To be a little boy is to be a little boy. To be sure. So?

That saying was nebulous to me, even as far as high school. I thought of it when I read Burns, "A man's a man for a' that!" I had no difficulty with that—a person is a human being for all his poverty or riches. Certainly to be little was to be little. Why repeat this as though it were something from the sayings of the sages of the ages?

Words can often serve to confuse and withhold meaning. Without punctuation or inflection they can appear as cloudy as a gray oblong blur. Often with manipulation or different inflection the same words may become contradictory and change meaning completely.

Albert Trunkel, who is the best minister in the conference according to many, came to Frankfort on his vacation to visit friends. He went to Calvary Church to hear Stone Parker preach. Brother Parker was busy shaking hands at the door, and Albert Trunkel left a note for him on the pulpit which read, "Albert Trunkel says Stone Parker is the best preacher in the conference." Brother Parker read it and then took out his pencil and put in a couple of commas and mailed it back to him. When Albert Trunkel saw the same note he had written, it read, "Albert Trunkel, says Stone Parker, is the best preacher in the conference."

"To be little is to be little"—that is the way my small

mind interpreted Nora's saying. Everyone nodded in profound assent. But I shrugged my shoulders in confusion, convinced that it had some meaning too deep for my understanding. I dared not ask, to open my mouth and remove all doubt about my ignorance. By not wanting to appear stupid, people remain stupid.

"To be little is to be little." So it was that one day when it was pride's day out, once again I pondered Nora's text. This time I went over to see Jeb. I tried to convey to him that to me these were words of sound signifying nothing. Jeb made no reply. He took pencil and paper and wrote down the expression for me to read. The words have been written on my memory ever since. Nora's words were wiser than they sounded. "To belittle is to be little."

To belittle onself is to be little. The world has yet to like the man who does not like himself. Think well of yourself if you wish others to think well of you. Reticence is the bushel that has smothered many a candle. Let the light of your ability shine. To hold that when God made you, he made a poor job of it, is to belittle God. Nature has its ways of trimming down the boaster and revealing his blandishments to the world. "Every braggart shall be found an ass." Life itself is a school of humility. Belittling oneself is no way of helping onself or the world.

Sometimes self-belittling is done to get credit for piety. Ezra Stump, who ruled his home like a tyrant and was a hardfisted man, said the same thing in every testimony meeting: "I am poor and weak and blind, less than the least of all saints. Pray for me that I may hold out faithful." Many such people belittle themselves to be exalted in the estimation of others; they do it to be thought of as holy. It is pride taking the form of humility. But people are not often deceived by this pseudo humility, and those who would seek recognition by belittling themselves only succeed in making themselves small.

One may disparage himself because he is starved for sympathy and uses this method of securing it. He becomes an infant with the language of the cry for the milk of human kindness. Soon the world finds him out for the baby he has become. He who has beggared himself becomes beggarly; he who disowns himself is disowned. It is well with proper modesty to think well of oneself, to keep clean, dress well, and walk the world with dignity. It is the man who quits on himself that the world also quits on.

One can always afford to be submissive in things that are of temporal or unimportant issue. So many of our differences occur at the point of small issues; so much ill feeling is generated over trivial incidents. In trifles over personal rights it is well to be humble. Assertiveness comes with better grace when the rights of others are in jeopardy.

Booker T. Washington came to Charleston for an appearance. His train was delayed, and there was scant time for him to reach the hall in time. He came out of the station to take a taxicab, but the driver refused to take a Negro in his cab.

"Very well," replied Mr. Washington, "you get in. I'll drive you."

He jumped into the driver's seat, and they reached the hall in time. He paid the white man and likely gave him some occasion to think about his prejudice.

Stone Parker was preaching on the theme "Love yourself." He was using as his text, "Love thy neighbour as thyself," making the point that one should love himself well, and his neighbor just as well. He rephrased an old saying in a way that seemed to say something: "If you could buy some people for what they think they are worth, and sell them for what they are worth, you could shortly become a wealthy man." So it is, to belittle oneself is to be little.

To belittle another's talents and accomplishments is to be little. It does not succeed in making the one criticized small, because envy is a subtle form of flattery. It only issues in atrophying the soul of the one who criticizes. Let no one be deceived—the judged one is not mocked; the mocker is. It may indicate that the critic recognizes himself as inferior and is endeavoring to trim others down to his stature. This is a folly, for it only works out to the end of making one even more inferior. To belittle another's qualities only makes one ridiculous in the estimation of other people.

To belittle another's handicap is to be little. One who uses such unkind epithets as "Hunchy," "Limpy," "Four Eyes," is as cruel as though he threw a stone. Words crucify as well as nails. To attack people who are crippled is a kind of hateful cannibalism.

Philip saw a boy running past and tried to catch him, but his limp gave him no chance; and the runners, taking their opportunity, made straight for the ground he covered. Then one of them had the brilliant idea of imitating Philip's clumsy run. Other boys saw it and began to laugh; then they all copied the first; and they ran round Philip, limping grotesquely, screaming in their treble voices with shrill laughter. They lost their heads with the delight of their new amusement, and choked with helpless merriment. One of them tripped Philip up and he fell, heavily as he always fell, and cut his knee. They laughed all the louder when he got up. A boy pushed him from behind, and he would have fallen again if another had not caught him. The game was forgotten in the entertainment of Philip's deformity. One of them invented an odd, rolling limp that struck the rest as supremely ridiculous, and several of the boys lay down on the ground and rolled about in laughter: Philip was completely scared. He could not make out why they were laughing at him. His heart beat so that he could hardly breathe. . . . He was using all his strength to prevent himself from crying.[1]

It is beastly to make sport of another's handicap. He who makes sport of another's lameness is himself more lame in mind. What primeval sadism it is to seize upon another's weakness and call public attention to it! It dwarfs the sadist. To belittle another's limitation is to make oneself small before the world.

To belittle another's faith is to be little. The ones who scorned the followers of George Fox as "Quakers," and who belittled the followers of John Wesley as "methodists," have become so small in time that history knows them not at all, while the ones they disdained have covered the earth. Faiths cannot be refuted by name calling. When we gravitate to the low level of employing scorn, we convince our hearers that we are bankrupt of sound reason, that we realize our own uncertainty, or that we are insincere. Epithets were used against one of our nation's greatest citizens when his opponents were unable to refute his principles. Cheap railings were used against the world's greatest citizen. He was called a devil, a glutton, and a drunk.

Brother Cross and Elder James had a debate at Harmony

[1] W. Somerset Maugham, *Of Human Bondage.* Copyright 1915, 1936, by Doubleday & Co., Inc. Used by permission of Mr. Maugham, Messrs. William Heinemann, Ltd., and Doubleday & Co., Inc.

one night on some religious phrase that I could give but will omit because it is irrelevant here, and nobody knows enough about the proposition to talk sensibly about it, much less resolve the question. Brother Cross was a giant of a man with long black beard and heavy hair. Elder James was a small man. As he began his presentation, Brother Cross looked over at the little man and called attention to his size.

"My little man, with a little salt on you I could swallow you whole," he said.

When Elder James replied, he said that while this personal reference was the poorest thing Cross had said, it was the best argument he had used.

"If Brother Cross were to swallow me whole," he declared, "he might have more brains in his stomach than he has in his head."

In the old debating societies a great deal of such interchange was used; little was ever settled. Epithets are epitaphs of deceased logic. If one has valid arguments against another's religion, let him use them in humility, always believing in the possibility of being mistaken. Vilification only shames oneself and stunts one's personality.

To belittle moral living is to be little. The pigmy personality makes sport of the rules of noble living and says, "It is nothing." Those who endeavor to live by codes of high ethical conduct he terms "holy Joes," "pious Willies." Such ones themselves are usually of small moral stature; quite often they are breaking the rules of clean living. They may be trying to make others as low as themselves.

Now, there is just as much gold on the opposite side of this coin. To belittle is to be little, while to make great is to be great. One about whom it was spoken that among those born of women there was not a greater than he, had the magnificent grace to say, "He must increase, but I must decrease." He was made great because he made his Master great.

We have followed a kind of outline on how to belittle oneself. The same pattern affords a method of increasing one's stature. To magnify another's talents and accomplishments is to reveal tall stature. To appreciate is to be appreciated. To emphasize another's assets and to "go the second mile" by endeavoring to cover up his handicaps is to stand tall and suncrowned. To exalt another's faith and to refuse to use derogatory remarks about that which is very sacred to him, is to rise above the common level. To elevate the codes of clean living at every opportunity, is to manifest height of character and to walk the world as a full-grown man and not as a midget.

How profound, then, Nora was, after I knew what she was saying! To belittle is to be little. Take this one along also, Nora. It belongs on the other face of the same sterling coinage: "To make great is to be great."

16

THE LUCK OF THE ROAD

It was on a rainy monday night. we had decided to stay in and work at our hobbies. We had gone to our gallery room, I to my easel and Suds to her ceramic table.

"Monday evenings are mine, to have and to hold. Other evenings you may give to others. You are to be my pastor on Monday nights. Promise?" That was Suds's premarital request, and love promised, though love has had a twist of a time trying to keep that promise. So through the years Suds's day follows Sunday, particularly the evenings.

Someone knocked on the door, and when I opened it, there stood a thoroughly bedraggled young lady, soaked from head to toe. She apologized and asked if she might come in and use the telephone. Her car had stalled because of shorted wiring. It had to be dried out, and what price dryness in this downpour! She called the garage for a tow truck, and after we had paid our respects to the weather, made small talk. Only one thing of that conversation has outweathered the years.

"Too bad to be unlucky on the road on a night like this," I ventured.

"I hope," she replied with a smile, "I shall always be able to take the luck of the road."

"Life is a tale told by an idiot," said one. "Life is a disease and everyone has it; the only cure is death," offered another. "Life is a vapour that appears for a little while and is gone," one writer suggested. "Life is a seeking after wind," said a wise king. "Life is a narrow vale between the cold and barren peaks of two eternities," ventured an agnostic. Life is a road, said the young lady.

A tale, a disease, a vapour, a narrow vale, a road—a metaphor is perhaps as good a suggestion in defining life as anything else. There is no use to employ long words and involved sentences and imagine that because you have spoken, you have said something. Life is only another word for something we understand all too little. It is its own greatest mystery story. We have more vocabulary than we have dictionary. Everyone is not only like Abram, going out and not knowing where, but also like Melchizedec, who blessed him, and was himself without beginning of days and without descent. What we cannot understand we are generally accepting and using, and this is sensible. We cannot explain the process of digestion—how a potato can become a man, walk the streets, greet friends, and perform the daily tasks—but we had better eat.

"I hope I shall always be able to take the luck of the road." Life is a journey, she suggested. We all travel it. When we take a trip, there are some things we have to think about. We had better get ready. It may rain or be clear; it may turn cold or hot; the way may be long or short.

If we are to face up to the taking of life's journey, there are some things we have to come to terms with. One of these is self. Our attitude will determine the road. Condi-

tions have something to do with it; the viewpoint has everything. As a man thinks, so his road will be. A second consideration lies in the fact that others are taking the same
road. Room must be made for them. They also want, and
will demand, their rights. Adjustments will have to be made.
Also, if we are going, we will have to pick up our pack,
"take up our cross," be prepared to carry our load, lend a
hand to others heavily laden; take our responsibility. If
someone has invited us to go along with him, to follow him
as guide and friend, we will have to have confidence in
his leadership, be willing to put our destiny in his hands.
We had better first make sure of our guide. If we decide to
go alone—and who knows the way?—we will be wise to
follow the road maps and watch for the waymarks.

Now, these may sound too simple to mention, but many
give too little thought to where they are going, what they
are taking along, whom they are following, and those who
journey the road beside them.

One day when we were walking through Jeb's orchard,
he picked up a red apple from the ground, broke it in two
between his strong hands, and gave me half. In his half lay
a worm, suddenly exposed to the blinding light of day.
"I imagine this little fellow is surprised," he suggested.
"People are often like that, all curled up comfortable like
in their small, apple world, oblivious of the tree, the orchard, or the light of another world shining down." Indeed,
many are; so busy with their little Winesap world, they
never seem to consider anything greater or higher; so engrossed with the outlook, they never consider the uplook.
Then, when suddenly their apple world breaks open, they

are shocked, surprised, and unprepared, hoping that if they just keep still, whatever it is will go away.

Once when Brother Hathaway had announced that he would preach on the theme "What is life all about?" he prepared to take a poll and interview people on what they thought life was all about; so he walked along Main Street and asked his question of several whom he met. Here are some of the answers: One said, "I'll bite!" Another, "What a silly question!" Asked a third, "Who cares?" One man said, "I never thought much about it." When he told one man that he was going to preach on "What life is about," he said, "Why don't you just stand up and say, 'Who knows?' give the benediction, and sit down?"

Life is a road; all are going along the same road. Few consider where they are going; thoughtless sojourners, no preparation, no map, no guide, "sheep having no shepherd."

"I hope I shall always be able to take the luck of the road." Well, to "take it" is no easy undertaking. A great many people crack up; state hospitals are crowded with lame-minded people who couldn't stand the strain. Some seek escape in alcohol and drugs. Some leap out of life's windows. Some buy jaunty little books and read slick articles that claim to have all the answers. Some attend cults that make exorbitant claims. For a while they dream in ecstasy, but the rough hands of the world rudely awake them again to reality.

"Take the luck of the road"; what she is saying is, I mean to face up to life's inevitables, to "take it" when there is nothing else to do. "Pick up your troubles, take up your burden, and go smilingly on," is an easy Pollyannagram; but if the burden you dropped happened to be your last dozen eggs, how can you? "Walk on, walk on," says a lovely song, but if you've had both legs blown off in battle, how then? "Always come up smiling," is no good for the man who has gone down for the third time. There are imperious compulsions in life. There is no escaping them; one must live with them.

Ed Smith had a lawn that was the admiration of his neighbors. He was working on it at every spare moment. Despite his efforts the dandelions were giving him considerable worry. They were gaining on him. In desperation he wrote several letters to the Department of Agriculture in Washington. They tried to help him, but apparently they too began to lose patience at his continuing importunity. They finally wrote to him, "We suggest that you learn to live with them." Certain things, we find, we must learn to live with; we must take.

Pain is inevitable. It is as much a part of life as living. Indeed, people generally mark their times by the notches of pain. Ask your neighbor when a certain event happened, and the reply may run something like this, "Let's see now. I was operated on that fall, and the following December was the coldest we'd had in years; Art lost his best brood mare that January; little Janice came down with the mumps, and in February our neighbor's house burned—furnace got too hot—well, it must've been around the first of March."

Look how many stanzas it took Tennyson to record his sorrow at the death of his friend Hallam. It was pain that produced this classic. Pain is productive. All the great children of culture and virtue are born with suffering. They could not be brought forth except by tears of blood and sweat of agony. So, pain is inevitable.

Loneliness is inevitable, even with the great number of people in the world. Situations isolate people. Greatness isolates people; it makes them prey to smallness, misunderstanding, and the thousand other things that mortal flesh is heir to. Loneliness is also the matrix of culture and progress. Out of aloneness Moses brought the Ten Commandments; out of aloneness came the Twenty-third Psalm, most of the great religions of the world, and many of the great inventions.

Life itself is the product of sorrow and pain. Man cannot at the first be born but by another's bitter pain; since then he cannot live without pain and death coming to something that must leave "the daisied dells and grassy murmurs of its peaceful ways." There are things that man cannot know until he has suffered. These things are the inevitables.

Blind Tom was as gentle a soul as ever blessed our town. No use to say to him, Keep your eyes fixed on a star. He had met one of life's compulsions. He had to accept the luck of the road. His eyes were set in darkness for life. One day going home he fell into a ditch near Hawkins' place. Cal came out and picked him up and told him how sorry he was for him. In telling about it Cal said, "He didn't seem upset much. Said some new things I hadn't thought about. Told me that I might be surprised to know that he often felt sorry for sighted people; said he'd seen things that people can only see in the dark. What things do you suppose?"

I suppose we who live in the light are also blind; blind to things that can be revealed only in the night. For one thing, in the light we follow our own sight, and as far as the future is concerned, that is next to blindness itself. In the dark we must follow God's sight. Tom had seen things people see only in the dark. The blind plowman sings of "God who took away my eyes that my soul might see." Maybe the dark is not as black as it has been painted. "The night has a thousand eyes," and they are revealed only when it grows dark and many of the myriads of stars are brighter than our day star. Likely they who "walk" in darkness, who go on, accepting the fate life gives them, see the great lights.

"I hope I shall always be able to take the luck of the road." It was a good thing to hope, but "always" is an ambitious wish. We are constantly vulnerable. She would be something approaching the unearthly if she could "always" take it, and not rebel, not fail. It is the privilege of the human being to fail now and then; the divine is not allowed to. Moses losing his temper, Elijah running into the wild wood for cover, Peter swearing like a galley deck hand; yet these have all come to be favorites of God and man. There are times when we do break. Let it be; weeping might endure for a night, but another day comes with the morning. He remembers our frame.

"The luck of the road." We can also have good luck. And even that which at the time may seem bitter as Marah, may, with the casting in of the branch of providence, become sweet as water from the well at Bethlehem. "I would ye should understand," said the man of Tarsus, "that the things which happened unto me have fallen out rather unto the furtherance of the gospel" (Philippians 1:12). This he said after beatings, stonings, jails, shipwreck, and all. So might we all testify if the complete evidence were in.

One day during the depression A. H. Graenser sat in the lobby of a hotel in Omaha. He had but five cents in his pocket. He had just been told that he could not re-enter his room to secure his baggage and overcoat until he had paid his bill. It was an embarrassing situation. He walked to the window and tried to see out, but it was all steamed over. This caused him to remember that an old German chemist had told him that glycerin soap rubbed on glass and wiped off with a cloth would prevent steaming of windows. At a nearby drugstore he bought a bar of glycerine soap with his last nickel. He sat in the park and cut it into twenty-four uniform parts. He called it "miracle rub." He sold the twenty-four cubes at ten cents each to gasoline stations for keeping windshields clean. Then he bought more of the soap and in the first day made twenty-seven dollars. He was in business. In three months he took a thousand dollars and formed in Detroit the Presto Products Company.

"Take the luck of the road"—who could refuse and know with full assurance that he was not willfully turning away angels bearing gifts, and was not shutting the door against opportunity, an opportunity perhaps to be richly used in golden service for fellow men?

"I hope I shall always be able to take the luck of the road." Consider the religion of this. Religion is simply saying, If God is God, he will vindicate his creation. It is a manifestation of faith in the basic, ultimate wisdom of things and a revulsion against the idea that all is nonsense. Nihilism is complete hopelessness. It is dry suicide. It is so flaccid that the robust soul finds it unworthy of acceptance. He will so live that if it be that ultimately there is no Eternal, or if the one that is refuse to vindicate the making of things as they have been, at least he has vindicated himself before the tribunal of his own soul. He will take the luck of the road. He will be the man.

"The road." We know not where it may lead tomorrow; but because we do not know this is no valid reason to assume that it goes nowhere at all. That the road is, is proof that it came from somewhere. All of our confusion is at the point of our doubt. We thrash about because we cannot know, because we must move along by believing, by faith. We try to draw conclusions from insufficient evidence. The insect cannot know that its home is being plowed under that a harvest might be; the bird cannot understand that its nest is destroyed that the tree may be used for building homes. It is like trying to fathom the ocean by measuring one drop of water, to judge a whole symphony by one note.

One solitary event, good or evil, cannot explain the whole of creation. Reverend Clarence Wells often uses a droll illustration. He depicts a parable of two insects. The first was born when the sky was arched in blue, the sun a golden radiance, birds in choirs, flowers abloom, and all like a paradise of serenity and peace. He lived his hour and died. The second came to the earth when it was saturated with gloom, sounding with thunder, flashing with lightning, and terrifying. He lived his little hour and died. Now, suggests Brother Wells, interview them. Get a dying statement. Ask them what life is all about. One will say, and the other will say. They will both have strong opinions. They will both be wrong.

"Let it rain," she smiled. "I hope I shall always be able to take the luck of the road." Indeed, "trust God: see all, nor be afraid!"